Jaki McCarrick

Jaki McCarrick won the 2010 Papatango New Writing Prize for her play *Leopoldville*, and her play *Belfast Girls*, developed at the National Theatre London, was shortlisted for the Susan Smith Blackburn Prize and the 2014 BBC Tony Doyle Award. *Belfast Girls* premiered in Chicago in May 2015 to much critical acclaim (Windy City Times Critics' Pick) and has since had numerous international productions.

In 2016 Jaki was shortlisted for St. John's College Cambridge's Harper-Wood Studentship for her short play *Tussy* about Eleanor Marx, a piece she is currently developing for Kibo Productions.

First published in the UK in 2018 by Aurora Metro Publications Ltd.
67 Grove Avenue, Twickenham, TW1 4HX
www.aurorametro.com   info@aurorametro.com

Cover image courtesy of Caitlin Cook
Production: Peter Fullagar
With many thanks to: Marina Tuffier and Angie Thorpe.

Printed in the UK by ImprintDigital.com, Seychelles Farm, Upton Pyne, EX5 5HY, UK

ISBNs:

978-1- (print) 978-1-906582-84-5

978-1- (ebook) 978-1-906582-85-2

The Naturalists

by

Jaki McCarrick

AURORA METRO BOOKS

Acknowledgements

The Pond Theatre Company would like to thank all of our supporters whose generous contributions enable us to introduce American audiences to the freshest and boldest new writing from the UK and Ireland.

Patrons

Erin Becker

Kate & Dan Belin

James Chanos

Jill & Daniel Clinton

Mary Cossette

Charles de Lardemelle

Michael DePalma

Anthony Dorment

Gail & Tony Ganz

Amy McCarty & Tim Mikesell

Chris O'Loughlin

Joanna Pozen & Anna Brenner

Carla Shen & Chris Schott

Mary Jo & Ted Shen

Sarah Steinberg

Betsy Witten

Michele Tall & Aaron Young

Anonymous

Champions

Marissa Alperin & John Lowe

Jonathan & Elizabeth Clinton

Dan & Linda Clinton

Jennifer DaSilva

Joan Dinowitz

Harriet & Richard Dorment

Melanie Fallon-Houska

Erica Komisar & Jordan Kassalow

Jennifer & Jerry Lee

Marion & Josh Panas

Cassi & Zachary Roth

Jennifer Russell

Nadine Topalian

William Vislocky & Cindy D'Luzansky

Malcolm & Maggie Youngrem

Partners

Mary Jo & Thomas Beagen

Eva Bonime

Keith Clancy

Maggie Clinton

Jennifer Clinton & Federico Glucksmann

Joseph Clinton & Andrea Liss

Jake Fisher

Joseph Franchini

Judy & Terrence Griffin

Eleanor & Jack Jaye

Aidan Keogh

Kate Koplan

Lindsay Lincoln

David Milazzo

Sal Monaco

Joan Nissman & Mort Abromson

Laura O'Loughlin

Mark Rosenblatt & Amy Abrahams

Goldman Sachs

Maura & Todd Sanders

Justin Sommers

Mary Battle Stump

Joan Wallstein

Barbara Wing

"Love is the every only god"

– E.E. Cummings

CONTENTS

ABOUT THE COMPANY

CAST BIOGRAPHIES

ABOUT THE PLAY

THE NATURALISTS

About The Pond Theatre Company

The Pond Theatre Company is an American home for British and Irish playwrights. We present US premieres of plays by emerging British and Irish playwrights and provide a context for those works through the revival of modern classics.

Founded by an international group of actors from the UK, Ireland and the United States, The Pond is dedicated to showcasing the work of playwrights whose work may have been produced in the UK or Ireland but who have had few, if any, opportunities to present their work to US audiences.

Co-Artistic Directors
Colleen Clinton, Lily Dorment & Sarah Street

www.thepondtheatre.org

The Pond Theatre Company

Cast

FRANCIS SLOANE	John Keating
BILLY SLOANE	Tim Ruddy
JOSIE LARMER	Sarah Street
JOHN-JOE DOHERTY	Michael Mellamphy

Production Credits

Jaki McCarrick	Playwright
Colleen Clinton	Co-Director
Lily Dorment	Co-Director
Chika Shimizu	Set Designer
Caitlin Smith Rapoport	Lighting Designer
Christopher Ross-Ewart	Sound Designer
Grier Coleman	Costume Designer
Ron Piretti	Fight Director
Julie Voshell	Choreography
Garrett Markgraf	Production Stage Manager
Melanie Aponte	Assistant Stage Manager
Josiah Parsons	Production Manager
Madeleine Goldsmith	Producer

Biographies

Cast

John Keating – Francis Sloane

Extensive New York credits include 6 shows with Theatre For A New Audience (most recently, Arin Arbus' *The Winter's Tale* and Sir Trevor Nunn's *Pericles* – also, *Much Ado About Nothing, Taming of the Shrew, Measure for Measure, The Broken Heart*), proud company member of the Irish Rep, where he has performed in 18 shows (recently – *Pigeon in the Taj Mahal, Rebel in the Soul, The Weir, Juno and The Paycock, Da*), Pearl (*Public Enemy*), Atlantic (*The New York Idea*), Mint (*Is Life Worth Living, John Ferguson*), Roundabout (*Juno and the Paycock*), Irish Arts (5 shows, including *Ladies and Gents*). Most leading Regional, including McCarter, A.C.T, Old Globe, Hartford Stage, Wilma (Barrymore nom – Best Actor) Television: *Boardwalk Empire, John Adams, Ray Donovan, The Following, Nurse Jackie, SVU, Alpha House, High Maintenance, Lipstick Jungle, On The Lig* Film: *The Lone Ranger, Emerald City, Freedom, Misty Button.* 160 Audiobook narrations – (Audie winner).

Tim Ruddy – Billy Sloane

Actor: *The Seafarer, The Weir, Stones in his Pockets* (Broadway Tour), *Philadelphia Here I Come, The Field, Defender of the Faith, Swansong* (IRNE best actor), *Prisoner of the Crown, The Shaughraun, The Yeats Project*, all at The Irish Repertory Theatre. *Pumpgirl* at Manhattan Theatre Club. *The Seagull*, directed by Max Stafford Clark at The Lynne Redgrave Theatre NY. *The Blowin of Baile*

Gall, Rockdoves (Irish Arts Center NY.) *MacBeth, Good Evening Mr. Collins, Shay* (Abbey Theatre Dublin). *Mrs. Sweeney* (The Project Arts Theatre, Dublin). *Look Back in Anger* (City Arts Dublin). *Wild Harvest* (Barnstorm IRL). *Translations* (Yolland. An Ghrinan IRL). Director: *AfterLuke/When I was God* by Conal Creedon and *For Love* by Laoisa Sexton (The Irish Rep), *The Beauty Queen of Leenane* (Actors Studio NY), *Last days of Cleopatra* by Laoisa Sexton (Urban Stages), among others. Television/ Film: *Glenroe* (5 Seasons), *Ballykissangel, Gettysburg, Gods and Generals, Making the Cut, WC.* Playwright: *The International* won best play at 1st Irish New York theatre festival in 2013 subsequently moving for an extended run at Playwrights Horizons NY in 2015.

Sarah Street – Josie Larner

Most recent theatre credits include, *Dyin' for it* – Origin Theatre Company, First Irish Festival, *Muswell Hill* – The Barrow Group/The Pond Theatre Company, *Rebel in the Soul* – The Irish Repertory Theatre, *Subprime*, New Jersey Theater Center, and New York Times Critic's Pick *Abigail's Party* – The Barrow Group/The Pond Theatre Company. She has also worked as an actor in TV, film, commercials and voiceover. Sarah also mentors students in playwrighting at Quinnpiac University, in Connecticut. She was recently nominated for Best Playwright at the 2018 First Irish Festival, for a short play she wrote as part of a site-specific production.

Michael Mellamphy – John-Joe Doherty

New York Theatre credits: *The Seafarer* (The Irish Repertory Theatre), *Guy Walks into a Bar* (1st Irish Best Actor Award 2018), *The Last Days of Cleopatra* (Urban Stages), *The Prophet of Monto* (The Flea Theatre), *After Luke* and *When I was God* (Irish Rep), *Dirty Money*, *The Guest*, *The Hairy Ape* (Irish Rep), *The Field* (Irish Rep), *Philadelphia, Here I Come* (Irish Rep), *The Cure*, (1st Irish Best Actor Award 2013), *Romeo and Juliet* (Petrolab productions), *In a Bucket of Blood* (Plays Upstairs), *King John*. Theatre credits in Ireland: *The Prophet of Monto* (Axis Ballymun), *The Agamemnon*, (SFX Theatre), *Purgatory* (RHA Gallery), *Oliver* (Cork Opera House), *Reign Man* (Cork Arts Theatre), *Mother Courage and Her Children* (UCC Granary Theatre Cork), *Brother's of the Brush*. (St Anthony's Hall). TV and Film credits include *The Good Wife*, (NBC), *Quantico*, (ABC), *Bartender Wars* (FLN), *The Hindenburg Omen* and *Living in Exile*. Michael has also worked as a voiceover actor for brands such as Tourism Ireland, Jameson Whisky and Paddy Whiskey.

Creative

Colleen Clinton – Co-Director

Colleen is an actor, director, playwright and a co-founder of The Pond Theatre Company. After graduating from The University of Michigan with a BFA in Graphic Design she transitioned to acting upon her arrival in NYC and has been working steadily in film, theatre, and television for the past twenty years.

Lily Dorment– Co-Director

Lily is a British actor and director and a co-founder of The Pond Theatre Company. She earned her BA from Yale University and her master's degree from Columbia University. She trained at RADA and at The Barrow Group. Recent credits: *Muswell Hill* (The Barrow Group/The Pond); *Abigail's Party* (The Barrow Group/The Pond); *Calendar Girls* (US premiere/ Ivoryton Playhouse) and *Platonov*, among others. Assistant Director to Seth Barrish: *Expecting Isabel* and *The Thing With Feathers* (The Barrow Group).

Chika Shimizu – Set Designer

Chika is a New York based set, costume, and projection designer. Her design credits include *Vietgone* (TheatreSquared), *Buyer and Cellar* (Bucks County Playhouse), *The Caucasian Chalk Circle* (Yale Rep, CT Critics Circle Award Nom. for set), *Romulus The Great* (Yangtze Rep), *False Stars* (Corkscrew Theater Festival), *The Seagull* (Access Theatre), *Assistance* (Joust Theater Company), *Twelfth Night; Or, What You Will, The Visit* (Yale School of Drama), *Don't Be Too Surprised, MuZeum* (Yale Cabaret), *Ching Chong Chinaman* (Artists At Play), *Romeo and Juliet, Tartuffe*, and a number of dance theatre pieces (Cal State Fullerton). Chika has MFA in Design from Yale School of Drama. She is a recipient of Donald and Zorca Oenslager Fellowship Award in Design.

Caitlin Smith Rapoport– Lighting Designer

Caitlin is a Brooklyn based lighting designer for live performance. Her recent work has been seen at REDCAT,

Yale Repertory Theatre, Theater Row, Ars Nova, Theater Squared, Cape Fear Regional Theatre, Totem Pole Playhouse, Soho Rep Walkerspace, The Wild Project, The Stonybrook Opera Company, Columbia University, American Academy of Dramatic Arts, at the Yale School of Drama, and on tour in Europe and the US with Wakka Wakka Puppet Theater's *Made In China*. This is her Pond Theatre debut. Upcoming projects include *Sister Selkie* with Dutch Kills Theater Company, *Turning 15 On The Road to Freedom* Produced by Miranda Barry, and *To Kill a Mockingbird* on Broadway (Associate). BA University of Massachusetts, Amherst, MFA Yale School of Drama.

Christopher Ross-Ewart – Sound Design

Christopher is a sound designer and composer for theatre and dance based in New York. Recent credits include the Rough Draft Festival at LGPAC, *Enjoy the Hostilities* (Toronto Fringe Festival), *Crowns* (Le Petit, New Orleans). He has worked across the US and Canada, as well as Hong Kong and Germany. He teaches sound design at the University of Western Michigan. He is thrilled to be working with this exciting team at The Pond Theatre Company.

Grier Coleman – Costume Designer

Off Broadway: *You're A Good Man, Charlie Brown* (York Theater Company); *Missed Connections: The Craigslist Musical* (The New Ohio); Regional: *Arcadia* (Yale Repertory); *A Doll's House, Part 2*; *All My Sons* (Weston Playhouse);*The Real Inspector Hound* (Theater at Monmouth); *MacBeth*, *Hamlet*, *All's Well That Ends Well*, and *The Two Gentlemen of Verona* (Shakespeare on the Sound); *The Parchman Hour* (Virginia Stage Company); *Disgraced*, *The Crucible*, *DOT* (Playmakers Repertory) Educational: Yale School of Drama, New

School for Drama, New York University, Washington College, Muhlenburg College, opera, dance, and drama divisions at The Juilliard School. MFA: Yale School of Drama. Member of United Scenic Artists.

Carrie Mossman – Props Designer

Pride & Prejudice, Discord, The Roads To Home, Fade, A Perfect Arrangement (Primary Stages): *Cry It Out, Airness* (ATL): *Out Of The Mouths Of Babes, The Traveling Lady*, 2018 Mentor Project (Cherry Lane Theatre); *The Effect* (Barrow St.); *Lost Girls* (MCC); *Hamlet, Faustus* (CSC); *Bright Half Life* (Women's Project Theater); *The Bandwagon* (NYCC Encore Series).

Ron Piretti – Fight Director

On Broadway, he has staged the fights for Sting's musical *The Last Ship, In The Heights, West Side Story, The Miracle Worker* with Abigail Breslin, *Bengal Tiger at the Baghdad Zoo* starring Robin Williams, and *The Performers* with Henry Winkler. He has worked as the fight choreographer for numerous productions Off-Broadway: *A Lovely Sunday for Creve Coeur, The Traveling Lady* and regionally including Goodspeed Opera House and Hartford Theater Works. As an actor, Ron appeared as Officer Krupke in the Broadway production of *West Side Story. The Traveling Lady* at the Cherry Lane Theatre. He has played one of the clowns in *The 39 Steps*. He currently teaches acting at The Barrow Group. He is one of the founders of The Performing Arts Project, a three-week summer intensive workshop in North Carolina. He received his MFA from the Goodman School of Drama.

Julie Voshell – Choreography

Theatre: Barrow Group productions of *The Pavilion, Origin-8, Fast and Fab, According to the Chorus, Letters to Sala.* Bubbles comedy night/ Nuyorican. Film: *Al B/ Eventually Z, Diva.* TV: *Diabolical, Shadow of Doubt.* As a dancer, Julie is a current member of Dances...Patrelle, and danced in the first national tour of *Movin' Out* under Twyla Tharp.

Garrett Markgraf – Production Stage Manager

Garrett has stage managed at The Elektra Theatre, Judson Memorial Church, Hudson Warehouse, and Target Margin Theater.

Melanie Aponte – Assistant Stage Manager

Past credits include Julie Taymor's *A Midsummer Night's Dream,* Billy Porter's *Ham: A Musical Memoir,* Michael Kahn's *The Metromaniacs* and John Rando's revival of *All in the Timing.* BFA: Rutgers University. Proud member of Actors' Equity Association.

Josiah Parsons – Production Manager

The Confession of Lily Dare by Charles Busch (Theatre for the New City) *Death of the Moon* (Jerry Orbach Theatre) *The Thing with Feathers* and *A Walk in the Woods* (The Barrow Group) and The Mentor Project (Cherry Lane Theatre). Other Credits include, National Tours: *The Illusionists: Live from Broadway, The Illusionists: Witness the Impossible,* and *The Producers.* Off-Broadway: *Jersey Boys, Here Lies Love, Peter and the Starcatcher, A Man's a Man.* Alumni of the University of New Hampshire with a B.A. in Theatre.

Madeleine Goldsmith – Producer

Madeleine is a New York-based producer determined to make art for our current political climate. In the last year, since moving to New York from San Francisco, she has produced works at Abrons Arts Center, HERE Arts Center, and Target Margin Theater. In the fall she will have productions at NYTW, The Bushwick Starr, SoHo Rep and Access Theater.

photo credit: Colleen Clinton

About the play

In 1979, on August 27th, the bombing of eighteen soldiers took place at Narrow Water, near Warrenpoint in Ireland, a few miles from where my family lived. Most of the press attention at the time went to another IRA atrocity that had taken place on the same day: the bombing of a boat in Mullaghmore, Sligo, which killed Earl Mountbatten and three others. Despite being less newsworthy than the death of a British royal, according to Tim Pat Coogan, the Narrow Water bombings were pivotal in Irish-British relations as the event which instigated the British policy of "Ulsterisation" i.e. keeping the problems of the North in the North – a policy which seems to have continued until today.

The central character of Francis is the "mastermind" behind the bombings. He is an entirely fictional character, as no one was ever charged for this crime. In Francis, I wanted to create a character with a past so dark that he could barely forgive himself for it. I also wanted to look at what such a crime does to the immediate family of the *perpetrator* and how, through the forces of nature and love, he and his brother, Billy, find their way back to some semblance of normality. It is the female character, Josie, who shows the brothers a way out of their past and in the brothers' difficulties, Josie herself, finds a renewed sense of purpose. At the end of the piece, Francis finds a way to embrace the spirits of the eighteen soldiers he killed by planting eighteen trees in their memory.

The play was first read in Ireland at the Flat Lake Festival in 2010, directed by Padraic McIntyre of Livin' Dred Theatre Company, with readings in the UK in London and Manchester before the current production.

– Jaki Mc Carrick

THE NATURALISTS

The Pond Theatre Company presented the world premiere of *The Naturalists* from 7th September to 23rd September 2018 at Walkerspace, New York City.

CHARACTERS

Billy Sloane – 40s
Francis Xavier Sloane – late-40s/early-50s
Josie Larmer – 30s
John-Joe Doherty – late-40s/early-50s

A stroke (/) denotes the point of interruption in overlapping dialogue.

Words in square brackets are not to be spoken.

Set in a rural hamlet in County Monaghan, Ireland, 2010/2011.

SCENE ONE

A mobile home, messy interior. Newspapers in piles, beer cans everywhere; window boarded up. Shelves are packed with books, some items in boxes: books, records etc. Picture of the Virgin Mary hangs over the electric fire; Jesus on another wall; also a crucifix and a picture of Saint Gerard Majella speaking to a skull; 'Angel' holy-water font beside door. TV, stereo. Door to mobile home is far upstage centre. Four small rooms off: two bedrooms, one box-room, tiny kitchen. (Toilet is in a shed outside.) The scene outside (seen when the door is open) is one of tall redwood trees and rolling hills, a distant lake.

BILLY SLOANE rushes in through the door, sits on chair by the table, takes off his Wellingtons, carries them back towards the door, waving smell, opens door, drops them outside. Comes in, rushes into his room, comes out, slippers on, jacket off. Rolls up shirtsleeves, puts on TV via remote control: EastEnders. Watches for thirty seconds. Goes into kitchen. Sound of running water and plash sounds as he washes himself at the sink.

FRANCIS SLOANE opens the door, takes his Wellingtons off at the door, turns and places them outside. Walks across the room, stops and looks down at his feet. He has just stepped in the cow-shit BILLY had brought in with him. He groans. On his heels, FRANCIS walks towards his own room to change. BILLY exits kitchen with a can of beer, sits on the sofa, opens beer, watches TV. FRANCIS rushes out, grab's BILLY'S beer, the remote control, puts TV off.

BILLY What ya do that for?

FRANCIS What I tell ya?

BILLY What ya do that for?

FRANCIS Told ya, didn't I?

BILLY But I was watchin' it. Give it here.

(FRANCIS puts the remote control and the beer on the table.)

FRANCIS Do ya not know how to live? We've just come in from one of the most beautiful nights of the year – and it's only May, Billy. May! We've the whole year ahead of us and, maybe, maybe this one'll stay dry enough for us to fix that house. So don't do the easy thing. The drink, the telly. And couldn't we leave the door open for a change and listen to the birds like we used ta? Oh, it's a beautiful night – and so warm, Billy ... *(FRANCIS opens the door of the mobile home and looks out.)* ... and the tall trees, the darkness of them against the still bright sky. Aren't we lucky in Ireland we have the long nights in May? We could be watchin' somethin' real, Billy, and not that oul shite.

BILLY What I want to be watchin' the trees for? What am I? A bird? Haven't we fecked our lives away on them long enough? I have anyway. You, at least, saw somethin'.

FRANCIS I saw nothin'! Leave it at that now. *(Beat.)* Just that ... we agreed. No beer. No drink till we've a meal on that table. And it's your turn. And ya did it again, Billy. What's with that, huh? Can ya not smell it? Jesus.

BILLY Smell what?

FRANCIS The half-ton a cow dung ya dragged in with ya fuck's sake. *(Beat.)* C'mon now. Dinner! It'll be the morra before we've had anythin' ta eat at this rate. I've done it all week, Billy. It's your turn!

BILLY reluctantly gets up, goes into the kitchen. A clatter in the kitchen as BILLY attempts to cook. FRANCIS looks for the mop, finds it and bucket in one of the rooms OFF, fills it with water from a tap outside the house, brings bucket in and proceeds to mop the floor. He occasionally stops to stare out into the fields, then carries on mopping floor. BILLY comes in and out from the kitchen into the room.

BILLY Look, we'll have to get some kind of a better set-up than this. Because, if we're not careful, we'll end up like those two yokes in the village, Jaxy and Charlie. Married to each other. And I tell ya something, I'll not be the bitch in the relationship.

FRANCIS Nor will I.

BILLY You sure about that now.

FRANCIS Shut up, will ya? *(Beat. Mulls over what BILLY has just said.)* Things you come out with. Jaxy and Charlie are old men.

BILLY Twenty years on me, a lot less on you.

FRANCIS Shut up!

BILLY I'm sick of the sight of ya.

FRANCIS Feeling's mutual.

Very long silence while BILLY carries on cooking meal. Long enough for the temperature to have cooled between the two men.

FRANCIS Blue skies today.

BILLY *(Off)* Aye.

FRANCIS Feels good to be working up a sweat in the oul sun.

BILLY *(Off)* It's all right.

FRANCIS Cows look like they're thriving in the low meadow.

BILLY *(Off)* Aye.

FRANCIS Calves growin' good too. *(Beat. No answer from BILLY.)* What ya cookin'?

BILLY *(Off)* Shite.

FRANCIS laughs lightly to himself.

FRANCIS Ya know, Billy, I was thinkin'. *(Slight beat)* Maybe, you're right. Maybe what we need is some help round here. Not with the fields like, we have them down pat – if ya pardon the pun – but in here ... until we get up to the house like. A woman maybe. Though what sort of a woman would take the two of us on and the devastation gets made between us, I don't know. No woman has that kind of tolerance or patience. There's not a woman I know 'd stick cleaning this place knowing the kind that lives in it. Unless she was mad. Or deaf to all she'd hear. Or blind to all she'd see. Or maybe all three.

The 'ping' of the microwave. BILLY comes in with two TV dinners. He has two forks in his pocket and sticks one into each platter. He shoves FRANCIS' dinner in front of him, shuts the door on the bright evening, grabs his beer and slumps onto the sofa and eats. FRANCIS watches this in disgust: look at our lives, he wonders ...

FRANCIS If ya don't mind, I'd like not to have the smell of shite in the room in which I am about ta eat. *(Gets up, opens the door, brings mop and bucket outside and leaves door open.)* Didn't I spend long enough in a room with no air, no natural light and the smell of shite for company?

BILLY No one asked ya ta fight for Ireland.

FRANCIS It wasn't for you anyway.

BILLY No. It most certainly wasn't.

FRANCIS Take yer boots off before ya come in next time.

BILLY I'll think about it.

FRANCIS You do that.

BILLY I will, aye.

FRANCIS gets up to reposition some of the pictures on the walls. Tilts his head this way and that to see if the pictures are straight.

FRANCIS It's the door, ya see. All the closin' and openin'.

BILLY Ya think because ya keep her holy pictures on the walls she's goin' ta come waltzin' back in here?

FRANCIS Not it at all.

BILLY Well, the day we see that woman again is when we're back up on that hill. Somethin' cookin', like money maybe, like the shop open maybe. Suddenly out of the blue, the bitch'll show up. Smiling, wriggling her way back in.

FRANCIS Leave it now, will ya?

BILLY And you'd be like no time had passed at all.

FRANCIS Ya don't know what yer talkin' about. As per fucken usual.

BILLY "Poor Ma" ya'd say, and ya'd fall at her feet like a faun. Well, not me. Get out of it ya dirty fucken oul whore is what I'd say. And I'd mean it, I tell ya that.

FRANCIS quickly picks up the remote control, puts on the TV, turns up volume then throws remote control to BILLY on the sofa. FRANCIS eats his food, slowly, deep in thought, staring out into the sunset.

FADE LIGHTS

SCENE TWO

A record is playing on the turntable: 'The Lark Ascending' by Vaughan Williams. FRANCIS is asleep in a chair. The door is open, a Sunday newspaper scattered about. Remains of a roast chicken on the table. FRANCIS is wearing a suit; his shoes are polished with laces undone.

Under the music the sound of a motorcycle engine. A woman (in her early to mid-30s), smoking a cigarette, comes to the door, motorcycle-helmet in hand. She is dressed in trousers, shirt, has her hair tied back. She stands at the door, peers in, takes in the disarray, stares for a long time at FRANCIS in the chair, listens to the music. Turns away, as if to leave – hesitates, stamps her cigarette out, then comes back, looks around again. Coughs – to alert FRANCIS. No answer. She bangs the door. No answer. Goes in, lifts the needle off the record, stands beside him. FRANCIS wakes up, slightly confused.

FRANCIS Ma? Is that ...?

JOSIE Sorry, Mr. Sloane, I ... I knocked but you ...

FRANCIS Oh, I was just ... you, you're ...

JOSIE I'm Josie.

FRANCIS Josie ... *(Beat.)* Oh yes. Josie. Indeed. Sit, sit, do.

JOSIE I can come back ...

FRANCIS No, no. Stay. Stay. *(Beat.)* So ... how's she keeping, your ... Moira?

JOSIE She's good. Busy.

FRANCIS She sounded it.

JOSIE Aye.

Slight beat.

FRANCIS Well, this is it, Josie. All what ya see. The temporary arrangement. Until we've fixed the house above, ya know? *(JOSIE nods.)* Ah, we do our best. But what with work and all we've ta do. So help is the ticket I think. Moira explain all that ta ya, she did?

JOSIE She did, Mr. Sloane. Aye.

FRANCIS Good.

JOSIE Ya've cattle, I see that.

FRANCIS Aye. But Billy's more the animal man. So ta speak. Billy's the brother. *(Slight beat.)* It was him got this yoke, in fact. From a couple in Newbliss. Building a house they were, and sure didn't we think we'd only be in it a month or two ourselves till we'd sort out the homestead?

JOSIE You didn't think of parking it up there? Beside the old house, maybe?

FRANCIS Ah, with the hill and all. And ya see beside us, the old shop? Here was best. For the shop, like. In the days it was open anyways.

JOSIE It's a good caravan though.

FRANCIS What?

JOSIE *(louder)* A good caravan.

FRANCIS Hmmm. It is. Aye. *(Slight beat.)* Well, as I say, we're busy Josie. The fields and the ploughing and the hay and all. And we've plans. Plenty plans.

JOSIE Moira said. *(JOSIE looks around, FRANCIS follows her gaze.)* So, how long are yez here?

FRANCIS Oh – about eighteen year.

JOSIE Oh. Right.

FRANCIS Ya see, we're not putting the time we'd like into the house up there, Josie, which is the whole point of, well – you.

JOSIE Though you can live well in a caravan, if you put your mind to it. That'd be my opinion.

FRANCIS Well, now, it's not actually a caravan, Josie. This, ya know. Not as such. Strictly speaking. I mean, we're not ... Well, what I mean ta say is, ya saw the shop out there, on yer way in?

JOSIE Aye. I saw that. Sort of ... old style ... with the corn-yellow ...

FRANCIS That's it. With the corn-yellow sign: 'W. Sloane Esquire: Hardware and Liquor'. A good shop one time, Josie. Once we were the only reason to stop at Swan's Cross at all.

JOSIE Once it was a fine establishment, Moira said.

FRANCIS Aye. She would remember.

JOSIE What happened?

FRANCIS Ah! People. Sure they stopped coming. Had their reasons, I s'pose. *(Slight beat.)* Anyways, it's a 'mobile home'. That's what I meant ta say. That's what we call these things nowadays. Though I don't know why. No one ever moves them from what I see. Caravan – well, that's another story. Different connotations. Not that it matters.

JOSIE No.

FRANCIS What am I talking about? Bad start. Would ya like a cup of tea? Wouldn't that be the thing ta offer a / a young ...

JOSIE Yes. That'd be nice. (*She sits into a chair, makes herself comfortable)*

FRANCIS Good then. I'll just talk across. That's how we do do it. Me and Billy.

FRANCIS goes into kitchen. There is a panicked clatter of cups and utensils – until FRANCIS becomes more self-consciously calm. The sound of the kettle boiling.

(Off – and talking across at JOSIE)

FRANCIS You met him at all – Billy?

JOSIE Couple of times. Once at a disco, in Carrick I think it was.

FRANCIS *(Off)* He was with the lads then most likely.

JOSIE Aye. That time.

FRANCIS *(Off)* All the times! Believe me. All the bloody times!

JOSIE Well, that's fellas.

FRANCIS *(Off)* Nowadays. Aye.

JOSIE I saw him another time at the bus station in Monaghan. He was there. Least I think it was Billy.

FRANCIS brings in the tea, places on the table.

FRANCIS Oh, she told me you were one for the travels. Moira.

JOSIE Did she?

FRANCIS Said you had an interest in dancin' too.

JOSIE Well, I do, but it'd be a certain type. Don't get the kind of dance I do round this way.

FRANCIS And what would that be now? Belly-dancing, maybe. Something different like that?

JOSIE Oh no, Mr. Sloane. I like, well I like most – what they call contemporary styles? My thesis was on the work of William Forsythe. Though I am more interested these days in the early pioneers, such as Isadora Duncan.

FRANCIS Oh, I see. *(Long pause as they drink their tea.)* So, Josie. It'd be just these rooms, the washing, some cooking, bits and pieces. Light housekeepin' I'd call it – though *(joking, awkwardly)*, not as in an actual lighthouse. Naturally! That'd be by the sea like. *(Beat)* Two, three days a week I'd say, wouldn't you? You see how it goes. And we agree a price. Reasonable but fair.

JOSIE looks around the room.

JOSIE What happened your window?

FRANCIS Billy. That's what happened.

JOSIE nods. Beat.

JOSIE You have a beautiful view, Mr. Sloane. The tall trees out that way. And it's quiet, too. Reminds me of the forests in Italy. In the North. Especially on the evenings we're having now. Aren't we lucky in Ireland that we have the long nights in May?

FRANCIS regards her more carefully.

FRANCIS Call me Francis, Josie, do.

JOSIE Well Francis, I'd bike it in from Ballybay in the fine weather, and in winter if there was snow I'd get a bus to Newbliss then a cab.

FRANCIS And is that a motorcycle ya have out there – with the hat and...?

JOSIE Aye. A scooter. A Honda 50 I have.

FRANCIS Not be one a those Hell's Angels now, would ya?

JOSIE No, Mr. Sloane. I'd not be one of those.

FRANCIS And no car?

JOSIE No.

FRANCIS Well, Josie – Moira, Moira's whole family, in fact, was very good to ours after ... she tell you things, maybe, Josie, maybe it's right and proper you knew?

JOSIE She told me some things.

FRANCIS Well, Billy is sensitive to things said. 'Bout me. 'Bout us all. 'Bout Sloanes in general. Take no notice is what I say.

JOSIE If you'd have me, that'd be great. But I'd be here to do a job. You see, I like to be out, Mr. Sloane. Francis. In the air. I could get a job in an office.

It was open to me, but for now it's not what I want. Here – well, it's close to the woods. I like that. And, I don't know, but you seem to have all the smells of the earth in here.

FRANCIS That's just shit, Josie. To put it bluntly. That's all that is. He does drag it in. *(She laughs. Beat.)* Look, we want to be gettin' on with that house up there. Time we got into it. We're not gettin' any younger, that's for sure. And sure, how can a life move on when you've two men in a confined space like this, huh? So we have ta try and get a move on. Me and Billy. And we could do with the help, Josie, ya know? So, if you'd be happy ta *(she nods. Beat)* ... well then, good. Good. And we – we have a spare room down the hall there. A box room. Not that ya'd ever need ta, ya know, Lord knows ... but if it came to it and ya ever wanted ... like if ya do take the job and find with all ya'v ta do ... like the journey would be a long one I'd say...so if ya wanted ta ... in winter or otherwise ... emergencies or otherwise ... it'd be there for ya. The room, like. Somethin' at least. Though you suit yourself. That's the ticket.

JOSIE Grand. There's just one thing, Mr Sloane – Francis.

FRANCIS What's that?

JOSIE I'm a – a vegetarian – well vegan now actually, so just regarding any food preparation/

FRANCIS Oh well that's fine, Josie. We'll be grand with that. Yer vegetables and the like. *(Enter BILLY)* Ah Billy! This is – Josie. She's Moira's ...

BILLY walks out to the fridge, grabs a beer, comes in, grabs the chicken carcass, sits down on the sofa, puts on the TV, eats straight into the carcass, and drinks.

FRANCIS She's come in hope of makin' a few changes.

FADE LIGHTS.

SCENE THREE

A week or so later. Window repaired. Curtain on window. Tidied up interior. A bowl of apples on the table and a vase of flowers on the coffee-table. BILLY enters, places a slab of beer on the coffee-table, moving the flowers out of the way. He's getting ready for the soaps. The mobile home door is open; the scene outside is the same – only warmer, brighter. Birdsong. BILLY looks for the remote control.

BILLY The vixen ... the little fucken ... where in Christ's name did she ... *(he finds it on top of the TV)*

He is about to press TV "on" when he hears voices outside – and laughter. FRANCIS and JOSIE approach and stop in the doorway to stare out at the view. BILLY tidies himself and removes the beer from the table, brings into the kitchen – or hides under the sofa, whatever is quickest. He peeps out at FRANCIS and JOSIE, tries to listen from the sofa.

FRANCIS This was all part of our grandfather's land. 'Estate' would be the word he'd've used, but we can hardly call it that now as so much was sold off. But all in front of you here is indigenous woodland. One of the few woodland areas in these parts to be left untouched. The lake to the right, Aiken's Lake, cuts to a winding stream that goes before those trees, see, the cherry and ash? Ya see, just ... aye, that's it – bend your head that way – towards that silver line *(FRANCIS goes closer to her. At this point, and because of the break in FRANCIS' speech, BILLY goes closer to listen)*, that's the lake thinnin' out. That's where the whole origins of Swan's Cross comes from, ya see. We're like a wee island up here, surrounded almost by that lake and stream. And swans would go by, under the bridge, against the grain of the road, sorta. And so you got Swan's Cross. Always in twos they are, the swans. Two's company, as they say. We keep a little boat down there and it used be a glorious thing to go out on a fine day when the water is still. Mother liked nothin' more than when father would take us all out onto that lake on a fine day. And beside us there, ya see the shop, "W. Sloane Esquire: Hardware and Liquor"? How fortunes change, eh? Oh well, it's a long story, Josie. Billy thinks we should bail out now, ya know? Sell up. This land'd fetch a pretty penny now he reckons, but he knows I'd not do that. I sort of see it as my role these days to look after it all, but that ... ah, it's a long story, too. Anyway, what I was saying there about the elements Josie, is that – in the same way the language we speak is composed by an alphabet, vegetable and plant production assumes the same enormous variety, in its forms and properties, by means of only a small number, maybe just over a hundred – elements. And together they compose, what we naturalists would call the true alphabet of the language of nature. All things, all the things ya see, are made up of these elements. The main ones being: Potassium, Sodium, Calcium, Magnesium, Silicum, Sulphur, Phosphorous, Chlorine, Iron, Manganese, Aluminum, Carbon, Oxygen, Hydrogen – and Nitrogen. That's it. Nature. You could sum the whole thing up in around a hundred and eighteen words. But like the alphabet, it's all about permutations and combinations. For instance, mix hydrogen and nitrogen together in the dark – there will be no combustion at all. But add to the mixture – sunlight – and you'll see an explosion take place immediately. *(BILLY puts on the TV and turns up the volume.)* Oh, Billy must be ...

FRANCIS and JOSIE enter the mobile home.

FRANCIS Ya see to that timber for the floor, Billy?

BILLY I did, aye.

FRANCIS Good. We'll have somethin' to walk on, soon enough then, Josie, hey? Up in the house. *(Slight beat.)* Josie's got a flat, Billy.

BILLY That's nice. Ballybay is it, or Newbliss?

FRANCIS Ballybay or Newbliss? What ya jabberin' about?

BILLY You just said, Josie's got a flat.

JOSIE He means on my bike, Billy.

FRANCIS Course that's what I meant.

BILLY Why ya tellin' me for?

FRANCIS Because she needs a lift, Billy. It's Friday!

BILLY You take her.

FRANCIS You know damn well I ...

JOSIE Look – I'll call a cab. It's no problem.

FRANCIS Billy!

BILLY OK!

FRANCIS Good then. Now, I'll need to sort ya. Give me two minutes.

(Gives BILLY a glowering look, exits towards his room. Beat.)

BILLY Like our view then?

JOSIE Aye.

BILLY S'pose it doesn't compare to those places you been ta, hah? Italy, Europe. Haven't ya seen all a that?

JOSIE Seen some of it, aye. And yes: this is as good as any of the places I've seen.

BILLY Must have been in some shite places, so.

JOSIE I was in beautiful places. Florence, Rome, Krakow, Naples.

BILLY And this holds up?

JOSIE It does. The trees there. The redwoods, the beautiful rhododendrons you have, and all the whitethorn in bloom as it is this time of year. People round these parts are all caught up in making money. None can see the beauty that's out there.

BILLY None but you.

JOSIE And Francis of course.

Slight beat

BILLY Should be gettin' a car, rather than that oul bike.

JOSIE I like that bike, actually.

Beat.

BILLY Been meaning ta say. D'ya mind not mixin' everythin' up in the place when yer cleaning it?

JOSIE I don't mix.

BILLY Well, ya do. Today for instance. I could hardly find the remote. *(JOSIE looks around, sees the remote control in BILLY's hand. BILLY clocks this.)* So. Had a week of us now. What ya thinkin'? That we'd be bad as old Jaxy and Charlie Gallagher – that old Irish cliché: two bachelor brothers gone ta fuck on their mammy's farm?

JOSIE No, no I don't think that. Besides, Jaxy and Charlie still ride donkeys. You at least have a car.

Pause.

BILLY I was a vet almost, ya know.

JOSIE Were ya?

BILLY Aye.

JOSIE What happened?

BILLY Did one year. Worked hard gettin' inta the college and all. I was good at Maths, see. A natural. Maths and biology. A head on me for all that. Calculating mind, ya know? But then Francis came home. Home from Long Kesh? *(Beat – to see if she knows this information)* And our Ma – well she, see she couldn't look after him by herself, as he was a bit, well, ya know. As anyone would be, I suppose, after spending that long in a place like that. That was it then, sorta, for the studies.

JOSIE So you came home for Francis? That was noble of ya, Billy. To do a thing like that for your brother.

BILLY Family isn't it?

JOSIE Family, aye. Never think of returning? To college?

BILLY Na. Sure, what I learned I use here. Know a few things, ya know? Things ya wouldn't need to be spendin' money on a vet for anyway.

JOSIE Not wasted then, that year?

BILLY Nope. *(Beat.)* And he's no thick, Francis. But I s'pose ya'v gathered that.

JOSIE I have.

BILLY Have ya?

JOSIE Aye, Francis is a kind and learned man. Talks to me about this place. The land ya have. The old shop. Told me all about the history of Swan's Cross. Told me bout Long Kesh prison too and the time he spent in it.

BILLY Well, he has two degrees, put it that way. English and somethin' ta do with the environment. Ecology, I think it was. And we've books galore aroun' this place.

JOSIE I see that.

BILLY So we're no oul cliché pair of thicks in the back a beyond. Nothin' to be tellin' other people.

Enter FRANCIS. He gives her an envelope with cash.

FRANCIS Now. Don't go spending it all at once, Josie.

JOSIE No.

BILLY *(Rubbing his hands together)* Right then. What's her nibs got on for us tonight?

FRANCIS *(Reasonably excited)* Vegetable stew. Looks good.

BILLY Oh fuck that.

JOSIE Sorry – 'her nibs'?

FRANCIS Now Josie, Billy didn't mean ta ...

JOSIE Do you mind if I just say a couple of things? Mainly to you, Billy.

FRANCIS Listen up now Billy, will ya?

JOSIE First, No, I don't be talkin' about my private place of work to people in the town. I only sit with my auntie Moira and praise the lovely land ye have here at Swan's Cross.

FRANCIS Did you say somethin' ta Josie / there...

JOSIE I tell her how Francis has taught me my vetch from my scarlet pimpernel, shown me the violets and the toadflax along the hedge and the wild raspberry. How he's pointed out the wild garlic ta me, and how to tell it by the star shape it has. All these things I lived with and never knew the names of. I tell her Francis is a good teacher. I tell her all about these things and we do talk about yez – but I don't go gossipin'. First, because there's nothin' to tell: yez don't do much other than farm, do yez? And watch the soaps, and bring shite into your own house from the fields. Secondly, because I'm not that type of person. So I'd appreciate it – Billy – if you'd not be so paranoid. But the thing I'd like to say most, is, other than I worked hard on that stew – ye have buck-all kitchen facilities after all, so I reckon I done well out there – did neither of you hear of Women's Lib? Because if yez did, you wouldn't be standing there talking about me in the third person – and calling me 'her nibs'. I'm doing a job of work. And I want to be appreciated for it. And if I hear the like of that talk again while I'm here I won't come back. Because I don't have ta.

Long pause.

FRANCIS Billy. Apologise to Josie. Now. Go on.

BILLY You do it. You do it first.

Beat.

FRANCIS I'm awfully sorry for any offence caused, Josie.

BILLY Aye. Right. Yeah. Well, I'll do it then. Now. The car. Come on if you're coming.

BILLY exits. JOSIE turns to FRANCIS. He holds out his hand as if to shake on his apology, she offers hers. They maintain eye contact. Exits.

BLACKOUT.

SCENE FOUR

A few weeks later. Outside the mobile home. Downstage. The mobile home is now to be entered by walking around side and in through front door. From here the side of the old house can be seen. Some headway has been made on the house, a new wall built. The redwood trees are to one side. The thinning stream coming off Aiken's Lake can be seen in front of the trees. More intense weather. Bright sun, bees, birdsong. Swans on the lake. JOSIE, BILLY and FRANCIS sitting at a table set outside the mobile home, finishing their Sunday meal. Both men more tidily dressed, FRANCIS in his Sunday suit, the jacket off; the mobile home is in good shape. BILLY has a mouth full of napkin. He was doing a scene from 'The Godfather', and is pulling the napkin out of his cheeks.

BILLY Ah, Brando. Now Brando, Josie, was su-preme.

JOSIE I liked him all right.

FRANCIS I thought it was Westerns you liked, Billy.

BILLY And Brando in them! Frank Sinatra called him 'mumbles', but the more Brando mumbled in Viva Zapata! the better I liked it. The more he made ya want ta listen. The more ya had to imagine, sometimes, what he was sayin'. That always seemed so much more real ta me. The half-caughtness of it all. Like the way in life ya don't catch most a what's going on. Not even in front of yer eyes. Things are only clear later. Rarely at the time. Brando knew all that very well.

JOSIE You should have gone into the film business, Billy.

BILLY Wasted my life round here, that's for sure.

FRANCIS Don't say that, Billy. Ya didn't waste it.

BILLY "I coulda been a contender!" *(JOSIE laughs.)*

FRANCIS This was a great idea I must say, Josie. 'Al Fresco'.

JOSIE As we have the weather.

FRANCIS You've hardly eaten a thing, though. Go on, have somethin'.

JOSIE No, no.

BILLY Leave her will ya? She's not hungry, man.

FRANCIS Must be warm. That's probably what it is. The heat. I've a few clean vests in there, Josie. If ya wanted a change outta that shirt.

BILLY She'd look grand in one a your oul specimens. 'Wife-beaters' they do call them vests, ya know? He has some great taste in fashion, eh Josie?

JOSIE The beer is enough, thank you both. *(Beat.)* Could we have some music, maybe, lads? Radio – or some of those old records you have in there?

FRANCIS Less of the old.

BILLY Francie, now he'd be musical. Used play a bit on guitar betimes, and on that piana in there. Francis, where's that old guitar? D'ya take that from the house that time?

FRANCIS No, I did not.

JOSIE Well, the piano is just behind us.

FRANCIS Oh, no. Don't even mention that contraption now Billy, will ya?

JOSIE I've already heard ya sing, Francis, come on.

BILLY Did ya? Where?

JOSIE Oh. Round the place. A fine singin' voice, he has. 'Lived in' I'd call it.

BILLY Aye, that's it. Like that fella. You used have his records Francie. Fella with the smoky voice was in the cage in that film, 'Dracula'. Eatin' up all the little flies he was. 'Oh Vladimir, oohhh, Mr. Dracula, I'm one of yours now Mr. Dracula. One of the undead.'

JOSIE It wasn't Mr. Dracula, Billy. It was Count.

BILLY I beg your pardon?

FRANCIS He's talkin' about Tom Waits. And he knows full well his name.

BILLY Like she says, ya know where the piana is. I think you'll be pestered til you do somethin'. Come on.

FRANCIS Ah no.

BILLY Come on, Smoky!

FRANCIS sighs. Goes into the mobile home, drags a chair to the piano, rolls up his sleeves to reveal a couple of tattoos on his arms, two swans, lifts up the lid, sits down. And sings and plays Tom Waits 'Martha' from the album, Closing Time:

Operator, number, please,

It's been so many years

Will she remember my old voice

While I fight the tears

Hello hello there is this Martha

This is old Tom Frost

And I am calling long distance

Don't worry about the cost.

Cause its been forty years or more,
Now Martha please recall,
Meet me out for coffee
Where we'll talk about it all.

And those were the days of roses,
Poetry and prose and Martha,
All I had was you and all you had was me
There was no tomorrows
We'd packed away our sorrows
And we saved them for a rainy day.

He stops abruptly, pulls down the lid of the piano.

JOSIE Oh, that sound! Terribly sad, Francis. But beautiful. And sorta profound too.

BILLY He used sing that to our Ma. When he came home. And she would ask him to play it. Remember that time, Francie?

FRANCIS Some.

BILLY Whether he wanted ta or not, she would have him play. He took a while to come back to himself, did Francis. What's this now he would say? 'I am not here at all but I am "stranded" inside myself.' A mighty strange thing ta say, I used think. *(Beat)* Our mother, Josie ... you see ... her name – was – is – Martha.

JOSIE I know.

FRANCIS has stood up and talks to them from the door of the mobile home.

FRANCIS She knows the whole damn mess from A to Z, Billy.

JOSIE How long now, she ...

FRANCIS Eighteen year in the Autumn. She'd be what now, Billy? Age-wise.

BILLY She'd be oul. Like Francis.

JOSIE Francis is not old! He's like the brown bears I saw one time in Italy! They look like they've been around forever, even when they're young as babies.

BILLY Ya hear? You're a bear now Francis. An *I*-talian brown bear.

FRANCIS She'd be in her 60s, Josie. Probably big orange hair now – and walking a pink poodle somewhere.

BILLY She'd not be lookin' after no poodle. Pink or otherwise. Women like Martha Sloane care for no living creature except themselves. *(BILLY gets up, paces, FRANCIS still by the door. BILLY grabs a bottle of beer, downs it quickly.)* Oh, but she loved ta be sung ta, aye.

JOSIE Well, I thought it was just lovely, Francis.

BILLY aims the bottle at the newly-built wall, throws it and it smashes. FRANCIS comes out.

FRANCIS Billy, relax! Please. *(Pause.)* Ya know what? I was thinking when we've fixed that house we might have horses.

JOSIE Oh horses would be fine. When the house is done ya'd have these fields freed up and horses would be the thing to have. Maybe in this field, or that one.

FRANCIS Ones saved from cruelty, like. From a shelter. Don't have ta ride them then. When the horses come from a shelter they say don't breed or ride them. /

BILLY Don't see the point in havin' a horse you cannot ride. /

FRANCIS You're just givin' them sanctuary sort of. Anyway, it was only an idea, Billy. Don't bite my head off.

BILLY Well I think you were tellin' her – Josie – about that idea and not me at all.

FRANCIS I was just talking!

BILLY Isn't that all ya do?

JOSIE Now lads! Billy, why'd ya throw that beer at the good wall ya've spent all morning repairing, huh?

FRANCIS Leave it, Josie.

BILLY I don't know. I was reminded. The song or somethin'.

FRANCIS Come on outta that mood, brother. Isn't it a fine day we're havin' and the spread that she – Josie's – laid out for us? You'd be insulting the girl with flingin' that drink, I tell ya.

BILLY Well – I'm sorry for that, Josie. But there's things ... Sure, you only know us a while, ya know?

JOSIE Well, who wouldn't miss their mother, Billy? And a woman like Martha Sloane, too. Wasn't she known to be a bright and charming woman? One fine day, sure ya never know. People turn up outta the blue all the time. I remember her myself. Vivacious always; and beautiful, so ...

BILLY Ah Jesus. Stop it will ya?

JOSIE stops talking.

Long pause.

FRANCIS Ya know, I was thinking – Billy – that we'd let a meadow go wild. Down in front of the house. By the lime tree. *(No reply from BILLY.)* What d'you think Josie?

JOSIE Which one's the lime tree?

FRANCIS One by the meadow.

JOSIE There's loads of trees, Francis, by the meadow. What's a lime tree look like?

FRANCIS The lime tree has the heart-shaped leaves. That's how ya know a lime tree. And by its pale timber and yella blossom.

JOSIE I see. Well I think, Francis, a wild meadow would be lovely by that lime tree.

BILLY Do whatever ya like with it.

FRANCIS Nothin' like a wild meadow. The buttercups and tall grass and the poppies, Josie, to walk through especially. Against your skin, and under your feet.

BILLY She knows it well.

FRANCIS Knows what?

BILLY How lovely a walk in 'a meadow of buttercups and poppies and tall grass' is? Sure didn't herself and meself walk through a meadow of that self-same description yesterda, lookin' for that calf?

JOSIE That's right. It was lovely, Francis.

BILLY Course, I went at a big strong pace with her. None of your dallyin' and lookin' at the barks of feckin' trees. Seein' as we'd ta find that calf and all.

FRANCIS And did ya?

BILLY Did we what?

FRANCIS *(Sarcastically)* Find the calf.

BILLY Oh, aye. We found it. Eventually.

Beat.

FRANCIS Yesterday you say?

BILLY Aye.

FRANCIS When I was in Dublin?

BILLY Aye. And it was a fine day yesterday. Really fine. Fine day here especially.

Beat

FRANCIS Well, good for you. *(Pause as FRANCIS stares out into the land.)* Ya know – Josie – the American Indians – or what's now called First Nation peoples, and rightly so – saw themselves as – 'keepers of the forest', and their way was ta leave no trace of themselves. Accordin' ta them, spirits lived in the trees and sent us omens of good or evil. Even in their fires they would use only wee sticks and twigs. And it's taken the white man this long to think that maybe the Indians had it right. That we are all just keepers of the earth. I do my best to teach this. Pass on the knowledge. Impart a sense of responsibility. I say to my students, 'nothing is sweeter than to know all things,' as the Italian naturalist, Aldrovandi once said. And then I add, 'but to know them is to mind them.' But sometimes it feels like pissin' in the wind, what I do, ya know? *(Looks at BILLY)* Look around ya, Josie. Ya can't move for the selfishness and destruction. Some of the children I work with seem to care. Some days. Maybe there's hope with them. I don't know.

JOSIE I'd say your work is appreciated more than ya think, Francis.

FRANCIS Ya think so?

JOSIE I do.

Short beat.

FRANCIS Well, go on have another beer, Josie. Do. *(JOSIE opens another beer. Pause.)* Oh my. Isn't the grass beautiful when it sways in the breeze? This way, that. So random like.

(Pause, as they all watch the grass together.)

JOSIE Aye, Francis. It's a lovely sight.

BILLY Spec-fucken-tacular. *(Long silence. BILLY drinking quickly.)* Inta Ballybay tomorrow.

FRANCIS That's good Billy. Need supplies.

BILLY That shop with their fuckin' snide insinuations. Always the same oul questions. What's happening with the house, the old shop, how can yez live like yez do. Sure you're no better than Jaxy and Charlie down in the village. Course, tis all through gritted teeth and smiles it's done.

FRANCIS Shut up now will ya'?

BILLY Martha McVey and William Sloane. Big house, 95 acres, shop. And look what it all came to. Him and me and a caravan. For want of a better word.

FRANCIS It's not a fuckin' caravan! And it – it's you has the snide insinuations!

BILLY I do not.

FRANCIS Ya do. And you choose your moments, too.

BILLY Maybe it's time she knew a thing or two.

FRANCIS Well, ya know what? She knows Billy. She knows. So there's no need for you to be snide. Comin' at things from a bloody angle always. She knows it's no one's fault but mine. The whole thing. The house, the shop, Ma – our mother – My choice. My choice. We all know I'm to blame. So leave it alone, huh? *(Beat)* Now. The wind is light and we're havin' a time of it. For a change, Billy! For a change! And aren't we, we of all people, two fellas livin' like pigs these long years in this kip, aren't we due a change, huh? Something fine and beautiful like this day? Oh – *(he has become emotional)* for Christ's sake! *(He starts to cry. Gets up – and walks off.)*

Long beat.

JOSIE Maybe I should get off home now, Billy, huh? Been a strange day. He's – the two of ya – well something has upset you both. Or are you always this [crazy]?

BILLY Not always, no. *(Beat.)* He just blames himself for all that happened. And twelve years in a place like Long Kesh is a long time. *(Beat.)*

JOSIE Soon, maybe, if you keep working on that house, you'll be back up there and out of this, Billy. You'll be livin' well. And who knows, maybe there will be horses and the shop again in time. Ya have so much going for ya here at Swan's Cross.

BILLY Right. Maybe I'll take to the other side of that wall, then lay down the timber. Could go on with that tomorrow.

JOSIE Well, maybe I'll stay tonight, so. If it helps Francis and you get a move-on, like.

BILLY I s'pose we could make some headway then, aye. *(Long pause.)* Ya know, most people would think it a strange thing for an educated young woman like yourself to go out of her way most mornings to work in this oul shack in the woods.

JOSIE I'm not most people.

BILLY I've noticed. You're a strange fish is what you are.

JOSIE Am I?

BILLY Aye. Francis always talked about how he got solace out here. Would that be you now, too, Josie Larmer? Looking to forget things, lose yourself. Or find yourself, maybe?

Beat.

JOSIE Where did Francis go?

BILLY Where he always goes. Down to Aiken's. There's a swannery down there and he watches the swans go out onto the lake. *(Beat)* Come on. We'll surprise him.

They exit.

FADE LIGHTS.

SCENE FIVE

JOSIE and FRANCIS and BILLY are on Aiken's Lake in the small boat. They have sailed out to the centre. It's evening and all is still and calm. FRANCIS has a prominent place in the boat.

FRANCIS All this beauty, Josie. Out here, this tranquil evening. You can see, though, how there's so much more than beauty, too, can't ya? An order. How everything is slotted into place in a way no human being could ever invent or design. The hills rollin' down to meet the water; the swans going by; that single oak in the water there; the pink-lit sky; the gravid centres of the butterflies skimming the surface; the sound of the lake lapping the rocks. All this – is what the poets and painters, composers and philosophers used refer to as: 'the sublime'. And sometimes *we* do see it, too. Sometimes, it is so utterly moving it's startling, and shakes me to my bones so as I cannot breathe. As if the very next moment it might turn – into something else. Something dark. And sometimes, it all just makes me feel sad. Because I know the moment will pass – and so will I. Ya do miss the sublime in a car. You might get the beauty all right, but you miss the spirit.

Because the spirit is out here – in the centre of the lake, or in the unbounded woods, or on the hilltops. And as you open yourself up to this quality, Josie, you begin to see and feel differently, so that it's almost like learning a new language; a language of close-seeing and understanding. Though you will find then that there are those who might not be in step with you in this, who might not sympathize with your love of nature. Because for them nature is a thing for sale, and everything in it has its price. So, when you find you can see the sublime as the artists and poets see it, you must also protect yourself. By seeking out people who also speak or understand your language. One other, I have always thought, is more than enough. Though you'd be extra lucky with two. It's likely everyone else will say you're mad.

BLACKOUT.

SCENE SIX

That night. The door of the mobile home is open. We can hear hammering in the distance, and there is a light from the hill. Inside, FRANCIS is flicking through some books that he and JOSIE are putting up onto a shelf previously hidden by junk and newspapers. JOSIE is wiping them with a cloth and handing them to FRANCIS, who is putting them back on the shelf. The hammering comes from BILLY, who is fixing the floors up in the old house.

JOSIE Could ya keep them in size-order, Francis, please.

FRANCIS Size order it is then! *(He sighs)*

JOSIE What?

FRANCIS Wonderful to see these old relics again. E.M. Forster, Thomas Hardy, Sam Hanna Bell ...

JOSIE Well, that's the point of a bookshelf. To see what ya have in the line of books.

FRANCIS In the Kesh there'd be times I'd be readin' these till four in the morning. When I'd not be able to sleep with all the thoughts goin' roun' my head. Reading and studying was a way to escape a lot of those thoughts. Keep me focused on the thing in hand.

JOSIE Concentrate Francis!

FRANCIS *(stops at a particular book, flicks through it)* Oh, this is a wonder.

JOSIE *(moves closer to FRANCIS to look at book)* What's it about?

FRANCIS A woman who defies convention in rural Ireland. Not an easy thing to do I tell ya, then or now. To my mind Sarah Gomartin is one of the greatest heroines in all of literature. You'd like her, Josie. Here. *(He offers JOSIE the book, she accepts.)* Now. There we are. All in a row. Just like a library. *(FRANCIS comes away from the books, goes to the door, looks out at the night. The hammering continues.)* He'll be at that a while yet.

Beat.

JOSIE You – you all right, Francis?

FRANCIS Ah, my thoughts. They just go off sometimes.

JOSIE To where? Oh – oh, of /course...

FRANCIS No, no Josie – it's fine. *(Pause.)* Just that – you're young. How could you know what it's like to be ripped out of a place as fabulous as this? Ta find yourself each morning, year after long year, facing nothing but cold tiles. In a way, you die. I died. I wasn't from the city, ya see, I'd not seen the pogroms or had my house raided like some of the other inmates. I'd come from this, all this, and I wasn't used to places with no air.

JOSIE But you're making up for that time now, aren't ya Francis?

FRANCIS There isn't enough time to make up for what I lost.

JOSIE No. I suppose not.

Slight beat.

FRANCIS And no man – even a former – 'activist' – can afford to have his mother just get up one day and vanish! Leave his life for good!

JOSIE She never wrote?

FRANCIS No. She told Billy one morning she'd had enough, wanted a new life in the sun. That's the last he saw of her. I blame myself of course. Blame myself entirely. *(Pause.)* Now – Moira, Moira knows the convenience of ya stayin' over? She'd be all right about that?

JOSIE Oh, of course. Late now, anyways. She knows I can't always be headed back to Ballybay. The inconvenience and all.

FRANCIS Good. Good. *(JOSIE lights up a cigarette and steps outside.)* Jesus, you can smoke that inside Josie. Not a palace ya know.

JOSIE It is ta me. *(She remains outside, smoking, her mind cast back to some uncomfortable memory of her own ...)* Don't they seem like a million years ago sometimes, those things of the past?

FRANCIS Aye, they do. Keep your eye on the thing in hand, that's what I do say now. And humbug to the rest.

Beat. JOSIE sees FRANCIS' jars of branches, herbs, seeds and feathers etc, by the door.

JOSIE What are all these Francis?

FRANCIS Oh. These are for the children. So that when term starts in September I'll have a good collection. *(He takes a branch from a jar, brings it to the table, under the light etc, JOSIE returns inside the mobile home to look)* This is from the Rowan; see the black buds? And this ugly thing here *(shows her another jar)* –is bog cotton – *(moves on to another)*; and inside here we have bluebell seeds. See? Tiny and black, like peppercorns. *(JOSIE looks, touches a seed in FRANCIS' hand)*

JOSIE You're like a wizard, Francis.

FRANCIS Or a witch, maybe.

They laugh. Slight pause.

JOSIE *(Goes to the radio)* Do you mind if I [put this on]?

FRANCIS No. Go ahead. *(JOSIE puts on the radio – showband music; she sways to the music. FRANCIS tidies up his jars.)* Do ya ... do ya go out much when yer home, Josie?

JOSIE Sometimes. Not a lot.

FRANCIS Oh.

JOSIE I'm still adjusting to ... from ... being away. I told you about my plans?

FRANCIS Of course. The dancing school.

JOSIE And I try to dance. When I can.

JOSIE dances more openly now, displaying a few moves. Balletic/contemporary – a bit rusty but FRANCIS is impressed.

JOSIE *(Stops)* I keep a scrapbook. Of my travels. In Poland and Italy. Sometimes I look through the pictures, imagining I'm there. Viareggio in the North, Naples in the South.

FRANCIS D'ya wish ya were there now?

JOSIE No. Everything is better now, Francis. Much much better.

FRANCIS Oh, that's good.

JOSIE Come on. *(She puts up the volume of the music, pulls him up to dance but FRANCIS is a block of wood).* Relax. Close your eyes and imagine something nice. The lake today. The peace, and the water back and forth. That's it. You're lighter now. Just follow me ... that's it.

They dance to the music. Suddenly FRANCIS stops abruptly, puts the radio off, turns away. JOSIE, slightly embarrassed resumes her jobs around the mobile home, laying out plates for breakfast etc. Pause.

JOSIE You never think of, maybe, leaving for a while, Francis, doing some traveling yourself, maybe? It might do you good.

FRANCIS Did my fair share, Josie. Different places. Hard for me to leave here now, though.

JOSIE I suppose, with the farm / and...

FRANCIS No. It's not that. It's hard to [explain] ...

JOSIE No, I sorta see...

FRANCIS Do ya? *(Beat)* Ya see – I think the more I stay here at Swan's Cross the more likely I am to find again the part of me I left behind when I was in prison. Because I've not found it yet, Josie. Not fully. Not fully at all. So I find it a difficult thing to be away from here for very long. Does that sound strange?

JOSIE No. Not at all. *(Long beat.)* Anyway.

FRANCIS What ... *(slight beat)* You said 'anyway' – like as if ya were goin' ta say somethin', somethin' else.

JOSIE Oh, no. Just I'm – I'm off to bed now, Francis. Been a long day. A brilliant day, too, I think. Thank you for the book. And the lesson *(referring to the jars)*.

FRANCIS I enjoyed the dancing, Josie. I did.

Sounds of the hammering. They listen for a second or two.

JOSIE Billy wants to get up to that house so much.

FRANCIS We both want it.

JOSIE Well, like you said. It's due yez.

FRANCIS Aye.

JOSIE Goodnight Francis. *(Goes to exit towards her room)*

FRANCIS Josie?

JOSIE Yes?

Beat.

FRANCIS You know, I'm not old Josie, I'm – just – a bit – What I'm sayin' is – I do have dreams and hopes of travel same as anyone else, same as Billy. We both – we just sorta both got stuck here. After I got out of prison, then when she went, and then waitin' for her to come back. Waitin' and waitin'. We had sightings. About forty sightings. We looked into them all of course, ya have ta. And we thought she'd be comin' home so many times. And she didn't. *(Slight beat)* But I'm still … in my heart I'm, I'm young. I didn't mean to get old. And there's plenty of places I would like ta see …

JOSIE You're not old Francis.

FRANCIS In fact, here and in here, I'd be about the same age as you.

JOSIE I know that.

FRANCIS The body gets … that's all.

JOSIE You don't have to [explain] … I'm a modern person. I've seen a lot.

FRANCIS Goodnight Josie.

JOSIE Night Francis.

FRANCIS goes to the bookshelf and pulls a book off the shelf, then another and another until he has a large pile in his arms. He goes towards his room, then doubles back to put out the light. The books fall to the floor with a thud. JOSIE comes out and sees this.

JOSIE That's a lot of books to be taking to bed, Francis.

FRANCIS Oh, I couldn't make up my mind.

JOSIE You must have had a lot on it anyway for that amount of books. Here. Let me help.

FRANCIS Oh no, there's no need at all.

JOSIE You being such an old man and everything.

They pick up the books, and both bring them towards FRANCIS' room, laughing – a particularly intimate, knowing kind of laughter.

FADE LIGHTS.

SCENE SEVEN

Later that night. The door of the mobile home is open. BILLY sits on the steps, reading a letter, his back to the audience, his dinner plate beside him on the floor. JOSIE rushes out of her room, goes to the kitchen, gets a glass of water, drinks it all down, puts the glass back on the table. Hangs over the table, very distressed, breathing heavily, shaking, scratching at her arms, wiping the sweat of her head. She doesn't see BILLY, who observes her carefully.

BILLY You all right?

JOSIE is startled. Beat.

JOSIE How long ya been there?

BILLY Hour. Why?

JOSIE Nothin'. Just, you'll catch your death.

BILLY Looks like you caught yours already.

JOSIE Had a bad dream, that's all it is. *(She picks up a rug from the sofa, wraps it around herself – JOSIE is always cold. Beat.)* Come in late did ya, Billy?

BILLY You monitorin' things like that now? Time I come in and all.

JOSIE No Billy. I'm just askin' a question.

BILLY Came in a while ago.

JOSIE How d'you get on with the floor?

BILLY Good. Just we'd want ta have no rain now. A few leaks up there, ya know?

Beat.

JOSIE What ya got there?

BILLY Nosy Parker.

JOSIE Right. Goodnight then, Billy. *(Turns to go)*

BILLY It's a letter.

JOSIE Oh?

BILLY For Francis.

JOSIE You've written Francis a letter?

BILLY No. No. Came for him. Days ago. I opened it.

Beat.

JOSIE You shouldn't have done that.

BILLY Well, it's a good job I did.

JOSIE Why's that?

Long pause.

BILLY Ya know, ever since you came, Josie, I dunno, but things have been all outta step around here. We work harder. More time for more work. I'm more tired yet I can't sleep. I don't watch the soaps. He goes round singin' in the fields. There's not been singin' in those fields since my Ma ... Anyways, what I'm sayin' is – from next week – it might be an idea for you to stay at home like, in Ballybay, for a while. Ya see, we're to have a guest.

JOSIE Oh?

BILLY Aye. You wouldn't mind that now?

JOSIE If that's what ya want. You and Francis.

BILLY Well, it'd be for the best I think. As it's an old friend of Francis comin' and all.

Beat. He returns to the letter.

JOSIE You don't seem too excited by the prospect Billy.

BILLY Don't I?

JOSIE No.

BILLY Well, maybe I don't like this particular friend. Maybe Francis won't be too pleased either. And I just need to figure out a way to tell him.

JOSIE Francis is not made of jelly! He's strong. Stronger than maybe you give him credit for.

Why wouldn't ya tell him? It's his letter isn't it? And what harm is an old friend comin'?

BILLY Keep your voice down!

(Hushed) It depends on the friend, obviously! *(Pause. Aware that he was harsh in his response he begins to elaborate.)* Look, you – ever – hear – of something happened – late 70s – '79 – August '79 to be precise – up by Warrenpoint, over the border? Place called – Narrow Water. You ever hear any stories or otherwise about the like a that?

JOSIE Narrow Water? Wasn't that ...

BILLY Aye. Biggest single blow ta – or massacre of – depending on your viewpoint – the British Army during the Troubles. Eighteen soldiers. Two trucks. Two bombs. Set off from deep in the Cooley Hills. In military terms, a perfect operation. Man that wants to come here – the old friend – come here and see Francis and me, is one of the men from that job.

JOSIE I don't understand. Why would a man like that be comin' to see Francis?

BILLY Why'd ya think, Josie? Why'd ya think? *(Pause.)* Ah, I see. Francis didn't tell ya the 'bombmaker' part of the story, then, huh? Aye. Your 'brown bear' in there – is – was – a leader of men, you understand? Yeah. Go too close to a bear he'll rip your fucking heart out and he'll not stop. *(Pause.)* In Long Kesh Francis made a deal. Not with the Brits. But with nature, the universe, God, whatever ya want to call it. That when he came out he would be this – naturalist. The naturalist he says he was born to be. A guardian of the earth, as he calls it. Gives talks in schools on trees and flowers and birds, he told ya that. Even said he'd get through the rest of his life without driving again. Just go about givin' back to the earth what he says he took from it. And not a drop of blood would he shed thereafter. He made that pact – and he's been good for it. So far.

Pause.

JOSIE Oh, you shoulda told me this before, Billy. Someone should. Moira.

BILLY Before what?

JOSIE Before I came inta yer lives.

BILLY Not something ya just tell people Josie, is it?!

JOSIE But ya shoulda told me! Ya shoulda told me it all!

BILLY How could I Josie, huh?

JOSIE Because this was meant to have been my prize! Ah ya don't understand. Neither of yez. *(Beat.)* Anyway, I'm not shocked. I'm not.

BILLY Ya should be.

JOSIE Though you might have told me before. It would have been nice to know. *(Long beat.)* It doesn't matter.

BILLY What ya mean, of course it does! Narrow Water is huge!

JOSIE I'm not saying I don't care. I'm saying, if ya thought you were shocking me, Billy, you're not! Whatever Francis did – it's what he believed. Then. He comes from a place of passion. And who am I to judge? He atoned. He's aton*ing*. Besides, none of us is white as snow, are we Billy? *(Beat.)* Spent a few nights in a prison cell myself once.

BILLY You did? Ya never said.

JOSIE I told Francis. Aye. Saboteuring. I temped once for Glaxo Smith Klein. Got information about animal testing on the premises and I passed it on.

BILLY Jesus. Where the fuck am I living at all? Colditz or someplace.

JOSIE Colditz? What's that?

BILLY Never mind.

JOSIE Look, I could be getting a car like you said, Billy. Make the commute to some town, put on a dress, take shite from some man in a suit, go out of my way to be what I'm not, forget about my dreams, my hopes to do what Isadora did – have my own dance group, right here, in my own townland, get the dance ideas from nature, like she did. But then I find this little jewel of a job in the woods, by a lake with swans, working for you and a man – a gentle, gentle man – who talks to trees! And it's only light housekeeping, like he says. Only a few days per week. And the two a yez are grand and kind and good to me. Well, most days. And now you say, stay away, because of something the details of which I'm not shocked by. So what are you protecting me from?

BILLY Look, I just owe this fella a few bob. So best you stay away till it's all cleared up. That's all I meant. *(Beat.)* Oh Jesus fuck. Ya know he *(points in direction of FRANCIS' room)* always wrecks it. One way or another, Always wrecks everything. And I'm tied to him like, like some symbiotic twin growin' out of his side.

JOSIE He's your brother.

BILLY Josie, Josie – I live here too, ya know? I'm here. I'm. Here. I wasn't in Long Kesh. I wasn't –political. I was in bloody college, and I quit! To be home, with her, waiting and waiting. Puttin' my whole life on hold. In fact, sometimes I think I'm invisible. That nobody sees me. So long in his bloody shadow have I been.

Beat.

JOSIE Well, I've not been here only for Francis, and ya know it, Billy, ya do. And there are times I think myself the luckiest woman on God's earth to be out here with such a complementary pair. One kind and thoughtful, the other – honest and strong – and certainly not invisible. Both different – and yet so fucking inseparable so as to seem the two halves of the one person. I been here for the two a yez, Billy. Always the two, and never the one, ya understand?

BILLY gets up slowly, takes JOSIE's rug and wraps it around her shoulders, continues his hold on both ends of the rug ... as he pulls her towards him.

FADE LIGHTS.

SCENE EIGHT

A few days later. The mobile home is almost as messy as in Scene One. JOHN-JOE DOHERTY ('Joey the lip') is lying out on the sofa, eating a TV dinner, drinking beer, smoking, watching EastEnders. There are a few newspapers strewn around, together with several screwed up beer-cans. BILLY opens the door, wafts the smoke in the room, waves the door, takes off his Wellingtons, leaves them outside, comes in, goes to his room, comes back out with his shoes on, jacket off. Looks at what JOHN-JOE is eating. Goes into kitchen, slams door. FRANCIS comes in, takes off his boots by the door, goes to his room and changes his shoes. BILLY comes in, takes a beer from the fridge, sits on the sofa, moves JOHN-JOE'S feet, grabs the remote control off him and turns up volume. FRANCIS comes out, goes into kitchen, comes back out and grabs remote control from BILLY, turns off TV and flings remote through the door into the field.

JOHN-JOE What ya do that for?

BILLY He's gone ravin'.

FRANCIS I have not gone ravin'. Seein' as, seein' as our friend there ...

BILLY 'Our?' Huh!

FRANCIS ... has decided to have a holiday at our expense, eatin' us out of house and home and wreckin' the house ...

JOHN-JOE 'House?' Huh!

FRANCIS ... we, brother dear, need to sort out what we're ta eat for our supper. So I need yer full attention while I ask ya if ya'd go in for a take-away ta Newbliss. Chips or somethin'.

BILLY Mullens is closed on a Thursday.

FRANCIS Jesus. D'ya leave us any food at all, John-Joe?

JOHN-JOE There's bread.

FRANCIS You were very thoughtful to leave us that. We could go mad on a bread dinner so. Two men out working in that heat comin' home to bread.

JOHN-JOE Please yerself.

FRANCIS *(Agitated)* Well let's see, we could have a bread sandwich. Two slices of bread with a slice of bread in the middle. It's a well-known speciality of mine.

BILLY We could do a bit a shopping, Francie. Shops open late up Ballybay way. Maybe – go in and see herself. Josie. See how she's keeping.

FRANCIS You hear from her?

BILLY No. No word.

FRANCIS Ah. It's as well anyway. With this fella here. How long you say you were staying, John-Joe?

JOHN-JOE Tell ya the truth, I don't know Francie. I didn't think you'd mind. Seems like there's room now your cleaning lady's gone.

BILLY She's gone coz a you. That's all. She'll be back when there's space.

JOHN-JOE Plus hotels are expensive places in Ireland these days, Francie. Ya'd need buckets a money and I don't have any.

(Glances at BILLY)

FRANCIS You think she'll be back, Billy?

BILLY Aye. I do.

FRANCIS Sure, I'll make us the sandwiches then. Live dangerously, huh? *(Exits into the kitchen, leaves door open)*

JOHN JOE gets up and walks about.

JOHN-JOE *(Primarily to FRANCIS, who is in the kitchen)* It's a restful place, Swan's Cross. Real restful. I remember you saying how restful it was, Francie. It was restful when last I was here too, only I'd forgotten. Put it outta me mind maybe. It was like this then. Warm. I remember that all right. Turned into a bit of an Indian summer that time. Martha was around then. Made me feel right at home in your new set-up. Oh, we had a time of it! Full a beans that woman. Wasted on this place, a course. Bone structure like that ya don't see every day, I can tell ya. Shoulda been in films, and she knew it. Oh ho! Husky voice like you do have Francie. Tear at your soul that voice. Well, ya shouldn't a brought a woman like that down here from the big house inta the damp fields, ya know? Ya hardly expected her ta stick around lads, did ya? Sure hadn't she left him a few times and didn't he always take her back, the oul fool. Tis only my opinion though. Don't mind me. Anyway – what was I ... oh yes ... it feels like I been here two, three weeks – when what's it been ...

BILLY Too fuckin' long.

FRANCIS *(Pops his head in, he can hear)* Few days. Billy, could ya make an effort, please, ta be a bit more polite? That's my friend there, eh? Eh, John-Joe? Joey the lip! S'pose you're still keeping up the fight, eh John-Joe? Squeezing the last juice out of it.

JOHN-JOE Oh aye.

BILLY War's over fella. 'Case you'd not noticed.

JOHN-JOE Is it fella? Well you'd be the fella ta have noticed that, I s'pose.

BILLY I would, aye.

FRANCIS *(Off)* It's called The Peace Process, John-Joe.

JOHN-JOE Aye. Emphasis on 'Process'.

Pause.

FRANCIS *(Off)* Ya know, John-Joe – you'd be surprised how many country children have never even held a bird in their hands.

JOHN-JOE And you get them to do that Francis?

FRANCIS *(Off)* I do. Last time out I found a swift and got one of the kids ta let it fly off a roof. A swift can't take off from the ground, and the children didn't know that about a swift. They do now.

JOHN-JOE They're lucky to have you, old friend. *(Beat.)* So how's it going up there in the big house?

FRANCIS *(Off)* Floors nearly done. Be up there in a few months I'd say.

JOHN-JOE You reckon?

FRANCIS *(Off)* Oh aye.

JOHN-JOE closes kitchen door a little as FRANCIS talks.

JOHN-JOE *(To BILLY)* I'm fuckin' watchin you.

BILLY I'm shittin' my knickers.

JOHN-JOE Ya'll be wearing them anyway, time I'm done with ya. You've this night and this night only to remember what you done with that money. Because if ya don't – well, put it like this: to begin with, I need a place ta stay. So if ya want rid a me ya better cough up. Show me the money, as it were. Because I know old Francie in there won't see me stuck. Will give me that back room. Maybe this whole caravan even, once yez get up ta that house – so as ya'd never get rid a me. Though you're makin' scant progress on it from what I can see. Take more than a few fucken months.

BILLY That's because we come home to a wrecked cara[van]... mobile home. Shit everywhere. No fuckin' food. We had a routine. A good routine. Had a girl come. And things were lookin' up. We were headed for that house just fine. Till you showed up. *(Beat. BILLY goes up to JOHN-JOE)* I. Don't. Have. Yer. Money. Told ya. I spent it. Ya said: look after Francie. And that's what I done.

JOHN-JOE I also said ta put some away for me, shit-for-brains. Till I got back from America.

BILLY What am I, a banker?

JOHN-JOE Close enough.

FRANCIS comes in with the sandwiches and tea on a tray. He hands JOHN-JOE a cup of tea also, who receives a glaring look from BILLY.

JOHN-JOE Ya know, I think I figured it out, Francie. Why exactly this place is so restful.

FRANCIS Yeah? Why so?

JOHN-JOE It takes so long to get here, that's why. Ya'd need a week's rest to get over it. No train. Not even a bus route. I checked.

FRANCIS Used to be track right through Monaghan, ya know? That was the daftest thing. Ripping that up. Getting rid of the trains. It's all car now, John-Joe. Carbon emissions, the whole lot. Road accidents sky-high. Road-kill everyplace. Hedgehogs, foxes, cats. How'd ya get here anyway?

JOHN-JOE Told ya. I hitched.

BILLY Who'd give you a lift?

JOHN-JOE You'd be surprised. I can be charming company.

BILLY That's once ya get in the car, maybe. But someone has ta stop for ya first.

JOHN-JOE Well someone did.

BILLY Obviously.

FRANCIS Shut up! Two a yez. Like a pair of effin' fishwives. You find this place restful, John-Joe, it's because it's quiet. I'd like to keep it that way if ya don't mind.

FRANCIS takes up his usual place at the table and looks into the bright evening. JOHN-JOE looks around, bored. BILLY eats his sandwich. Long pause.

FRANCIS So where'd ya go after the States, John-Joe?

JOHN-JOE England.

FRANCIS What ya do for money?

JOHN-JOE America or England?

FRANCIS Wherever.

JOHN-JOE Tried my hand at a lot of things, Francis. Found I had a talent for Sales. When I was in Sales I found I had a talent for stories and got put in the direction of a producer. A producer of films if ya don't mind! But that didn't quite pan out. *(Slight beat)* So – to cut a long story short – I eventually found myself in England. And I tried to get a job in the BBC ...

BILLY stops eating his sandwich and looks at JOHN-JOE completely incredulously. FRANCIS is nodding away, interested in all JOHN-JOE has to say. JOHN-JOE sees BILLY's reaction and puts a bit more power into the delivery of his story.

JOHN-JOE Researcher job I tried for. And I got it.

BILLY Researching what?

JOHN-JOE This and that. They do like the Irish at the BBC. Place is crawling with them. *(Beat.)* Anyway. I'm sorta unemployed right now.

Slight beat.

FRANCIS Ah well.

BILLY Maybe we should head inta Ballybay all the same, Francie. If Josie comes back, he'd have to head off then.

FRANCIS Quit now, don't be so rude. Guest and all. *(BILLY goes out the door, starts rummaging around in the grass.)* What ya doin'?

BILLY I want ta be watchin' TV as soon as possible – so if ya must know I'm lookin' for the remote you threw in the grass. Chucking good electrical equipment inta the fields. You'll be throwin' your own shite out the window next thing.

JOHN-JOE starts laughing. BILLY moves further into the grass.

FRANCIS I mean it now, John-Joe. Nice ta see ya, been a long time and all that, but what ya doin' here now, huh? All's different. As you can see. I'm not that fella went inta Long Kesh. Not by a long shot.

JOHN-JOE You're not. I can see that.

FRANCIS I'm glad I done those twelve years, do ya hear me, boy? Glad. I deserved it. I made somethin' of me time. I learned and studied.

JOHN-JOE Sure, everyone knows that, boss.

FRANCIS Jesus, don't call me that man! Not ever, ever again. I'm no boss. Not of nothing. We're out here. Farm. House – well, half a one. And workin' hard too. *(Sighs.)* Not a day goes by I don't think of it.

JOHN-JOE Nor me, Francie.

FRANCIS So why'd ya come here, huh? A fella like you? Likes the big times. Fond of the glitz and the big snazzy places. Why here? To Swan's Cross? You can hardly say you were passin' through, huh?

JOHN-JOE I just came, see an old pal, that's it.

FRANCIS So you say. We both done our time. Maybe we shoulda left it at that, ya know what I'm sayin'? *(JOHN-JOE nods)* I see you and I can't help it. I see that day up in Omeath.

JOHN-JOE Ya don't have to talk about it.

FRANCIS I do. Because – I'd convinced myself it was someone else done that, not me at all. Well, it was definitely me. Some a their faces. I remember them. From the binoculars. Close up. Young skin, fresh – and so fuckin' stupid. And as out of their natural habitat as fish out of water. The wee lad at the back lookin' out at the land. Watchin' his eyes I was. I remember those eyes, fighting the strength of the sun. And then *(makes a 'prrrhhh' sound, like an explosion)*. Blown sky high. In the middle of some of the most beautiful land in the Western world. A tranquil day. A warm day. Oh god, we were so bloody wrong. Those boys. Those boys.

JOHN-JOE Look at ya man! You've turned into a right oul fool out here in the backwoods. They were soldiers. And we were soldiers. End of.

FRANCIS Maybe for you. But not for me. Not for me, John Joe. *(Shouts out to the fields)* You find that yet, Billy? *(No reply.)* I served twelve years. I got eighteen, as ya know.

JOHN-JOE Deals were made./

FRANCIS / They were. But I would often smile at that number. Because I'd a been happy to serve eighteen lifetimes had they given me them.

JOHN-JOE Well, you were the mastermind.

Pause. FRANCIS does not like to be called that.

FRANCIS Now. We're fixing that house up on the hill there, and we've plans. Me, Billy and Josie.

JOHN-JOE Who the fuck is Josie? The maid? How's the maid anything ta do with it?

FRANCIS She's more than that. A whole lot.

JOHN-JOE In what way?

FRANCIS She's clever and good fun and there's a strength to her. Calls me a bear ya know. A brown bear. She's a dancer. *(JOHN-JOE clears his throat, sarcastically)* Though not the kind you do mean. Wants to open a dance school. Teach the 'liberation of body, mind, and soul' through movement. Isn't that somethin' now?

JOHN-JOE Oh, aye.

FRANCIS She loves this place. Says she gets great ideas out this way.

JOHN-JOE Maybe she's a gold-digger.

FRANCIS She's not a fucken gold-digger!

JOHN-JOE Aye. She just loves ya for ya good looks.

FRANCIS Never said anythin' about love, did I?

JOHN-JOE Ya didn't have ta Francis.

Pause.

FRANCIS How'd you find him, John-Joe? Billy I mean.

JOHN-JOE Yer askin' me, Francie?

FRANCIS Aye.

JOHN-JOE Why?

FRANCIS I don't know. He seems different these days.

JOHN-JOE Billy had it tough here with herself, ya know that.

FRANCIS I know. But it's all, I don't know, comin' to a head now or somethin'. Like he's becomin' a man at last and his old skin won't fit him no more.

JOHN-JOE Sure he's over forty years of age.

FRANCIS I know. But there's been – gaps – 'arrested development' some do call it.

JOHN-JOE Must be a woman so.

FRANCIS Ya think?

JOHN-JOE I do.

Enter BILLY with the remote control. FRANCIS mulls over what JOHN-JOE has said.

BILLY So am I leaving John-Joe inta the bus at Monaghan in the morning or amn't I?

JOHN-JOE Are these me marching orders, Billy?

FRANCIS Suppose we've a job to finish, John-Joe, and if we don't do it now it might never be done. I'll call Josie later and tell her we'll be getting back to business as usual. Been mighty havin' someone here ya can talk ta about things that matter. *(JOHN-JOE grunts upon hearing this)* Hey Billy? *(FRANCIS checks BILLY's reaction)* I'll tell her coast is clear. Be good ta see Josie.

BILLY Aye.

Beat.

JOHN-JOE Never heard from herself then?

FRANCIS Who's that now?

JOHN-JOE Martha. Your mother, Francis.

FRANCIS No.

JOHN-JOE Now, she – was a sassy one.

BILLY We do get up early John-Joe. Best ya get off on the first bus. I'll leave ya down there in the car.

FRANCIS It's a complete mystery, John-Joe.

JOHN-JOE Well, it happens. People take off everyday. Leave it all behind them.

FRANCIS But we were full-grown. I'll never understand it.

FRANCIS stares out at the land, thinking about the past.

JOHN-JOE All the more reason.

FRANCIS Where did she go ta at all, huh? How'd she live. It'd haunt ya, ya know? A thing like that.

BILLY There's a bus at 8.30am, another at 9. Though the first one is an express. That'd be the one to get.

FRANCIS But you don't even know where he's goin', Billy!

BILLY I do. He's goin' outta here. That's all I need ta know. And one a those buses'll take him.

Turns the TV volume up. He and JOHN-JOE watch TV and drink beer. FRANCIS stares out at the land.

SCENE NINE

Next morning, breakfast, table is a total mess, BILLY is very eager to get rid of JOHN-JOE. He paces, checks his watch, JOHN-JOE is v-e-r-y s-l-o-w-l-y getting himself ready, bags scattered about. He does not seem like a man in a hurry to go anywhere, and keeps checking his jacket ...

FRANCIS John-Joe, would you like something for the journey? Packet of biscuits maybe? Rich Tea – nice and plain? Let's see what I can find. *(EXITS to kitchen).*

JOHN-JOE pauses by the view.

JOHN-JOE What are all those pink flowers about the place, Francis?

BILLY Jesus. Who gives a fuck about it?

FRANCIS *(Off)* Rhododendron.

JOHN-JOE They're beautiful.

FRANCIS *(Off)* A lot of environmentalists don't think so, John Joe. Think they're a scourge on the landscape, dominatin' native plants, blocking the light and so on. Beautiful on the outside, dark and twisted underneath.

JOHN-JOE What do you think?

FRANCIS *(Off)* I think the rich pinkness of them worth it. Brought over to these parts a hundred years ago from India. Those botanists brought colour to these bland islands, ya have to hand them that.

JOHN-JOE Aye. I see why you stayed here. The beauty. The peace. The fecundity.

BILLY OK. Let's go.

JOHN-JOE Actually Billy, I'll not be going anywhere.

BILLY You will.

JOHN-JOE Will I be? *(JOHN-JOE pulls a gun. A substantial hand-gun – such as a Glock 17. BILLY jumps back.)* Relax. Everything can go real easy from now on. Now, obviously ya don't have the money I give ya. The actual notes like. It'd be no good anyways now we're in the Eurozone and we weren't when I give ya the money. So this is what we do. I want ten thousand / –

BILLY I don't owe ya that / ...

JOHN-JOE Today. By the afternoon. Hail, rain or shine.

BILLY How fuckin' dare ya. That's Francis Xavier Sloane in there. He was somethin'. A real leader. What were you? Nothin'. A.N. Other. Foot-soldier. And look at ya now? Ah ya fuckin eejit, get out, I don't have yer money.

JOHN JOE shoots the repaired window, making an almighty racket. FRANCIS open his door slowly, though it creaks loudly.

JOHN-JOE Come on out, Francis. I'm not gonna kill anyone. Not yet anyway.

FRANCIS *(comes out slowly, carefully)* Did ya really have to pull a gun on us, man? After all we done for ya? Whatever ya want we don't have it.

JOHN-JOE What ya mean? Ya've a hundred acres out there. Cattle, and a big fuckin pile up there.

FRANCIS Aye, that's it. A pile. A pile of stones.

JOHN-JOE Tell him ... ya big mammy's boy, go on! Tell him!

FRANCIS looks at BILLY. Pause.

BILLY He gave me money that time.

FRANCIS What time? What money?

BILLY When you came out of Long Kesh! I dunno – money from robberies, banks, post-offices, whatever. He gave me it so that when ya came home, whatever ya needed, whatever we needed – we'd have some help. You understand? They were your friends. Your people. They were helping you. But he also asked me keep something over for him. For when he'd come back here.

FRANCIS Billy, I wouldn't a wanted that. You know how much I wanted ta be free of ... Oh ya shouldn't have touched their money. Not for me, not for anything. How much?

No reply from BILLY.

JOHN-JOE Tell him how much you sarcastic fucker, tell him.

BILLY Ten.

FRANCIS Ten what?

BILLY Ten thousand a course!

FRANCIS What you do with it ... *(No answer.)* What ya do with that money, Billy, huh?/

JOHN-JOE My point exactly, Francis! /

FRANCIS Because you sure as hell didn't spend it on me. On us. Look at this place! Ma ended up here! With you. With you and no shop. Didn't she take off because of it?! Billy! Billy! *(Pause.)* What the fuck did ya do with 10,000 pounds? Like 40,000 now so it would be. What ya do with that kind of money, Billy? Billy! Billy!

There is the sound of a motorbike engine closing in on the mobile home.

JOHN-JOE What the fuck is that?

BILLY It's no one. The postman. Best put your gun down, John-Joe or things could get fucking messy.

There is a knock on the door then the sound of keys being jangled.

JOHN-JOE The postman has keys now, has he?

FRANCIS Listen you moron, put that gun down right now and we'll sort this.

BILLY *(calls out)* Go home, Josie!

JOHN-JOE indicates (at gunpoint) for everyone to be quiet. JOSIE comes in. JOHN-JOE kicks the door closed behind her then whacks JOSIE on the side of the head. She falls to the floor.

BILLY No! No! Josie, Josie. Don't hurt her. Please, don't hurt her! Please!

He cradles her, checks her head. FRANCIS looks on worried for JOSIE – but shocked and surprised by the tender care shown by BILLY towards her.

BLACKOUT.

SCENE TEN

BILLY is cleaning JOSIE's head wound with a cloth or sponge, a bowl of water beside him. It is a slow, sensitive action. And for a few seconds there is silence between them; the drops falling from the sponge into the bowl are clearly audible. The door is open.

JOSIE Where was I?

BILLY Naples. You'd gotten to Naples.

JOSIE Aye, Naples. The sticky heat of the South. The markets. The men playing draughts in the street. The ease. The peace. The sense of time standing still. ... Ouch!

BILLY Sorry.

JOSIE That's where I ... *(Long Beat.)* Ya see, something like that was never meant to happen to me, Billy. I'd not even taken a drink until I was 18. I'd studied hard, worked, trained, showed up for class on time. Always. Yet it did happen. *(Beat.)* It wasn't just the [drugs] ... it was me. My body. My chemistry. And it was as if, all my life, until that first hit, I'd not known that about myself. As if I'd been asleep to what I'd been made of. I was a dancer, I should have known. But it's like what Francis told me about the elements that are quiet together in the dark, asleep to each other, sorta, but once they hit sunlight ... *(Beat.)* How could I know that about myself? *(Beat.)* Anyway, I was working with this company – and I, I had to drop out. Of the thing I loved most in this whole world, I had to drop out. *(Beat.)* Naples was my flop-house of choice for about two years. You know how I quit? This woman found me and locked me in a room for several weeks. An ex-nun. A Poor Clare. When I came out, she looked after me. I started to jog. Manically. Every day. Just to use up this mad energy I had inside me. She saved my life. *(Beat.)* I used to hate junkies, ya know. They made me sick. I had no pity. Now, well I feel enormous pity for anyone who gets caught out like that. By themselves, by their own strange chemistry or design.

BILLY But why come back? To this place? Why didn't ya go to London or Dublin?

JOSIE I thought about it. When I first came home I used walk round Ballybay as if I was in some kind of coma. I swear I was that low my breathing slowed down. Then I came here. And in the most unlikely place, I felt the sun on me again. From you, from Francis, from Swan's Cross – from my being needed. *(Beat.)* Though when you told me about Narrow Water, the details ... those soldiers, those trucks... when that bastard's letter came, I admit, I panicked a bit.

BILLY I didn't think you'd come back. This wouldn't a happened only ya did.

JOSIE Like I said. I have pity, Billy – for the frail and fallen. Francis called me. Told me to come. And I remembered the promise you said he made. Sometimes – don't we need other people to have faith in us in order to keep our promises?

Sound of a car pulling up outside.

BILLY Just keep to the side of the room there. He can't hurt ya if he can't reach ya. *(She gets up, moves to the edge of the room.)*

BILLY opens door, throws contents of the bowl out. JOHN-JOE comes in; gun in his hand, points FRANCIS in, who doesn't look at BILLY. JOHN-JOE is carrying a plastic bag full of cash.

BILLY *(To FRANCIS)* Did ya get him the money?

FRANCIS Aye.

BILLY Well, what's he want now? Why's he back?

FRANCIS He wants ta use the toilet.

JOHN-JOE I can speak for meself, Francie, ya know? You're not the boss now so you keep remindin' me, so stop speaking for me, will ya? *(To BILLY)* I want to use the toilet. And I want the car. All of a sudden the thought of travelling on a bus with 10, 000 big ones on my person did not appeal. I felt the need of a car. Your car.

FRANCIS I tried to explain how much ya need the car, Billy, but he wouldn't listen. The car OR the money, I says.

BILLY Was the bank all right?

FRANCIS It's our money isn't it? Though the house fund is cleaned out now and we've a loan against the land to pay. *(Slight beat)* Looks like we'll die in this mobile home one way or another. *(FRANCIS sees JOSIE awake and alert in the corner. He quickly goes to her and checks her face.)* Yer a brute John-Joe! Take the car, the money and fuck off. Toilet is outside, as ya know. Ya need the other one though. The chemical one. The main one is blocked.

JOHN-JOE Sure, that chemical one's no more 'n a bucket!

FRANCIS Ya want ta use it or don't ya?

JOHN-JOE Aye.

FRANCIS Go on then! And good riddance. Leave us now. *(JOHN-JOE roars with laughter.)* What ya laughing at?

JOHN-JOE Look at youze two. She has ye wrapped roun' her little finger. She must be a mighty good cleaner, boys. Must have something real impressive in her. In those two little hands maybe. Obvious what's going on here, yez bloody fools. *(Laughs. JOHN-JOE thinks he's very clever.)* Isn't she doin' the two a yez? He loves her, you love her. She must have some slippery quiet feet the way she can slip around this caravan ...

BILLY This mobile home.

JOHN-JOE This 'mobile home' – if ya don't mind ... *(carries on what he was saying)* if she can be dupin' the two a ya and neither of ya guessing she's carryin' on with the other! Ah Jesus! It's better than any soap any day! Jesus, ya must be some actress, you. Small wee rooms. Wool pulled over the other's eyes. *(Pause.)* What? Are yez not bating each other black and blue over it? Two brothers? Sure half the murders in America are committed by brothers. Usually over money or a woman. And here yez are, and she's obviously doing ya b ... *(Pause.)* Oh. My. God. *(Pause.)* Yez know. Yez both know. It's fuckin' worse. It's fuckin' rich. It's fuckin' incredible. The two a yez know. Hang on, hang on, hang on. *(Beat)* That's immoral, that is. Two men, one woman. That is immoral. *(JOHN-JOE waves his gun around a lot during this)*

FRANCIS Morals? Do ya even know what one is?

JOHN-JOE Course I know. And this definitely isn't it!

FRANCIS And that gun is I s'pose?

JOHN-JOE He owes me.

FRANCIS Morals is it? Morals are nothin' but the customs of the people around ya, and conforming to those customs. If we were all vegetarian it would be immoral to eat meat.

JOSIE It is immoral to eat meat.

JOHN-JOE What's she sayin'?

FRANCIS Nothing *(diverting attention)*. She's a vegan. *(Beat.)* Look, there's no rules of the road out there. Not anymore. So how do ya live? Ya use the only thing ya can. Best compass a man has. Only compass a man has. His own heart. And we been using it, ya understand? There's no immorality here, other 'n you. Because you're all blocked up, John-Joe. Block up a man's heart – the way we were, up in Omeath, in those Cooley Hills that time, watchin' those young fellas across the water, watchin' their red cheeks and spotty faces and not feelin' a thing, well, that's the dead zone. And it looks ta me like you still live there. In that immoral place. Time for you to go now, John-Joe. After ya use the bucket, go on. Fuck the hell off.

JOHN-JOE Well, well, well. Ya know what youze three are? Pagans. Pagans doin' yer own thing out here in the backwoods. Heathens, pagans – whatever ya call it. All followers of the goat god, any road.

BILLY The goat god? What the fuck is that?

FRANCIS I think he means Pan.

JOHN-JOE That's him! Pan. I saw all about the cult of Pan on Sky. Is this what Swan's Cross does to ya, man? All a those trees? Well I seen everything now. Out here in the backwoods in this get-up. This oul trailer, like they do have in parts of America. Only those trailers'd be a cut above this thing that's for sure. In fact, I saw yokes like this in the swamps of Louisiana filled with folks on the run from somethin'. Real backwoods people hangin' out in 'gator country. Bad teeth, close-eyed, big-eared. And even those trailers were a cut above this thing. So the way I see it now, yez are turned half animal. Fallen in with the beasts of the field.

BILLY Well, in with some shape of an ass anyway.

JOHN-JOE You *(JOSIE)* get over here. *(JOSIE looks around her)* I said get up! Move! And get over here. Now!

FRANCIS Now what are ya doing, John-Joe? Don't ya think ya'v battered enough women for one week? Nearly took the eye outta the poor girl's head.

BILLY You lay a finger on her ...

JOHN-JOE And ya'll do what? You forget boys – I have the gun here. And I know there's no other gun in the place as Francie has gone all eco and shoots at nothin' these days. So relax. Stop panickin'. Who says I'll do a thing ... *(indicates for JOSIE to get up. She walks towards him)*

JOHN-JOE Though I must say, it's a very pretty eye. And I'm glad it's still in there. Lets have a look. *(He moves in closer to JOSIE, points gun at her head, moves her to the door)* Shame you turned inta such a shit, Francis. Ya used ta be – what's this word ya used use – 'scintillating'. You used be 'scintillating' company. Now you're mad as a March hare. So this here is the deal: I'm thinking that if I take her with me, say, least half of the way, least until I'm certain sure I'm COMPLETELY OUT of Deliverance country, that she'll be my little insurance policy against either a youze gettin' any bright ideas. Like callin' the cops and such. With the object of both of your affections in my car, now that it is my car, Billy, I reckon you'd be more disinclined to put her – and therefore me – at risk.

JOHN-JOE moves towards the door, points at JOSIE to get ready to move. At this, JOSIE moves up to him in a flirtatious manner, glancing at BILLY, hoping he will intuit that she 'has a plan' (to stall for time) and will intervene...

JOSIE Ah, but Mr. Doherty, before we leave there's something I should explain ta ya. Ya see, I – *(looks at BILLY, urging him to jump in during this speech)* I sorta – *get* – the two a them, and they me. It's as simple as that. Do you understand what I'm sayin ta ya? And really, you're in no position to judge us now are ya? So, in all fairness, I'd prefer if ya went alone in that car. After all, I'm rather partial to this backwoods trailer and the fellas that do live in it.

Suddenly BILLY lunges in, overpowers JOHN-JOE; the gun falls to the floor. FRANCIS picks it up, points it at

JOHN-JOE – who is on the floor being picked up by the scruff by BILLY.

FRANCIS Go easy, Billy! *(BILLY keeps punching JOHN-JOE)* Leave him! Get off him!

JOSIE pulls BILLY off JOHN-JOE, who is now flat on the floor. FRANCIS moves in on JOHN-JOE with the gun. We see a very different FRANCIS. He presses down his foot on JOHN-JOE'S neck. Opens the gun, checks the bullets, spins the barrel. He grabs JOHN-JOE up in one scoop of his hands, and flings him on the sofa. Grabs the bag of money, flings it at BILLY. Takes the car-keys from JOHN-JOE's pocket and slaps them on the table. JOHN-JOE fixes his bloody jaw.

JOHN-JOE He-hey! That's him. The old ghost! Francis Xavier Sloane! Ya see that, Billy? You – young one, Josie, that was him! Oh, aye. Up in Omeath. Precision, precision. Born quartermaster, IR [A].

FRANCIS lunges in with a roar, thinks about shooting him, instead punches JOHN-JOE in the stomach, turns away shaking. After a few seconds, JOSIE moves in and puts her hands on FRANCIS' shoulders. FRANCIS has paled, as if he wants to be sick.

JOHN-JOE Oh dear. Maybe he can't face it, huh? That maybe, this priest of the land shit is just one big lie; a hidin' place. Maybe that's it Francie, eh? Well, no wonder ya went mad when ya came outta Long Kesh, Francis. You're wired funny. And then there's Billy. Havin' ta look after Martha and then you. And him only a gossin. And what that woman wouldn't ask a fella to do for her.

BILLY Shut up! SHUT THE FUCK UP!

JOHN-JOE Sure I seen it plain as day with my own two eyes when I came ta this caravan. Didn't I, Billy? I was sent to check the place out ya see. Make sure it was fit for our top man, hey Francis? Round '92 I believe it was. Martha'd be drunk, sleep all day. Billy'd be cleaning up. She'd give ya this sob story about marryin' too young and how she needed ta get out at night, have 'male company'. Oh, yes! The bars of Ballybay. Must be the eighth wonder of the world that many bars in a town with only one street. But true as god, no son should have ta do what Billy did for that woman. *(To JOSIE)* You gettin' the picture here, young one? Martha Sloane was a deadbeat. And when she had no more use for ya she moved on. Oh, that one was passing through from the beginning, I'd say. Never meant to get stuck at Swan's Cross that's for sure. And certainly not in this contraption! Told me herself. Right there in that back room. Said if she didn't get out some way she'd bloody-well throw herself in the lake. And who would miss her, tell me? There are cats better mothers.

FRANCIS That's enough now John-Joe! E – nough!

JOHN-JOE What did she ever do for youse except stick all this voodoo on yer walls, tell me? And take whatever she could outta your father and you? And yez think yez'd have learned your lesson with loose women after your own mother feckin' off? No. Now the two of you have gone and shacked up with one! And only the one, mind you! Good God almighty, shoot me quick in case the weirdness of it all is catchin', for I'd rather be dead than end up like any a you shower of fuckin' misfits.

FRANCIS There's two bullets in this gun. But that's all right, because as you might remember John-Joe, you yourself used call me One Shot.

FRANCIS lifts gun to aim – hesitates. JOHN-JOE relaxes defiantly on the sofa. FRANCIS turns and shoots the TV.

JOHN-JOE Oops. No more soaps, One Shot. No more soaps for me and Billy. Poor wee Billy. Who ya left to do everythin' around this place for your poor loose mother. Her shop gone, her house a hape a stones, her husband dead, her legendary beauty somebody's memory. And alls she had ta look forward ta was wipin' the arse of a mad son home from Long Kesh. How the mighty fall, eh? From 'W. Sloane Esquire: Hardware and Liquor' – to this. And she had fallen, boy. She. Had. Fallen. Straight into the bed of her own son.

Silence.

FRANCIS maintains aim. He thinks, what the hell is JOHN-JOE saying! BILLY starts to cry. FRANCIS fumes and paces about, tries to get BILLY to straighten himself up.

FRANCIS Billy, come on, get up! *(Agitated, rapidly)* Why didn't ya keep some a that money Billy? Huh? Enough ta be givin' him when he came for it, huh? Ya don't cross fellas like that. He's Joey the Lip, Billy. Joey the Lip, because, because he'd never let a thing lie, Billy. He'd chew and chew and worry a thing ta death. Like some sort a ferret or pole-cat that'd have to get what he came for and that's it. Oh Billy! All the mess ya've caused now. It shoulda been over. It shoulda all been over. *(Gets to the point)* What does he mean by it! What is he sayin'?! Talk ta me! Talk ta me will ya!

JOHN-JOE laughs.

FRANCIS *(to JOHN-JOE)* Now you shut your filthy mouth. Our mother wasn't well. She'd a lot to put up with, ya hear? You shut your filthy mouth. You shut your filthy mouth.

BILLY I didn't spend it, Francis! The money. I didn't ... Not a dime. Do ya under ...? Do I have ta spell it out ...? I'd gotten in touch with a doctor in Dublin. For you. He reckoned what ya had was – a, a – cocktail of – trauma and grief and guilt. He said he could help. Get ya ta talk, move on. Get ya ta not be – so, so – stranded – in yerself! And she knew this. She knew what that money was for. She knew well. We'd talked about it. She'd stroke your hair and tell ya how things would get better in no time. How everything would change. What we'd all do. Get you well. Get back up to the house. Start up again. Together. And then, one day I came home from the fields. You were out, down by the swans most probably – oh, but she, she had gone with ...

FRANCIS So she took the money! Fine! But it's that other thing he said. What does he mean by it Billy? What does he mean? *(Pause. BILLY keeps sobbing. To JOHN-JOE)* Listen, whatever you thought you saw the time you were here before, ya were mistaken. My mother was never ... Billy was never ... she was eager ta have a good time, a good life, aye. But she was never perverse. Alright? She was never perverse.

JOHN-JOE But who says it was her idea though, eh Francis? I was here long enough to get the full oul sordid picture.

BILLY Tell him ta shut up, Francis! Tell him ta shut the hell up! You have the fuckin' gun now man. Do somethin' about it! Do it! Do it!

FRANCIS is shaken by this. Seems frailer than before, a little dazed, points the gun but his hand shakes.

JOSIE Francis, you can't do that. Look what you're asking him to do, Billy! Francis made a promise, remember? Francis made a promise!

FRANCIS *(still pointing gun)* Talk to me, Billy, talk. Or so help me I don't know what I'll do next.

BILLY What John-Joe saw was right. But he knows nothing. That night – when I – wasn't I near enough having a breakdown, crying I was always, with the amount of care and work, broken with it, and alls I went into her bed for was hugs and cuddles – and hugs and cuddles is all I got *(screamed at John-Joe)* – ya hear me –

Hugs and cuddles. hugs and cuddles. hugs and – fucking – cuddles. She was my mammy. And I – . And I miss her, the fucken bitch. I miss her. *(BILLY cries)*

JOHN-JOE Oh dear! Oh deary deary dear. If it isn't' the brothers grim. He's made some sorta vow to the goat god – and this one misses his mammy. Jayz, I think I could probably lie here on this sofa all day now insultin' the two a yez. Maybe havin' a go at yer missus there in the back room. Maybe take over the whole fucken caravan establishment. And ya'd still be standing there, Francis, not knowing what ta do with that gun. Cross wires ya see, cross wires.

JOHN-JOE laughs, goes towards FRANCIS, mocks him, and is about to take the gun, which FRANCIS continues to aim when JOSIE moves in and grabs the gun. She aims and shoots JOHN-JOE, who falls back onto the sofa.

BLACKOUT.

SCENE ELEVEN

This scene occurs in moonlit darkness. There is no speech here and the scene should have the effect of a silent movie. (Soundtrack that might be played here: Mark Lanegan and Isobel Campbell's 'Keep me in mind Sweetheart'.) A car approaches off-stage. The car headlights dim, the car door shuts. The silhouettes of three men enter stage right. Two men (FRANCIS and BILLY) are dragging JOHN-JOE across the width of the stage. They will end up stage-left; the drag should take two and a half minutes (length of the Lanegan/Campbell song). FRANCIS has many crises during this time, stops and cradles JOHN-JOE. BILLY is steelier, determined to drag JOHN-JOE along. Occasionally, BILLY lifts JOHN-JOE. BILLY has to console FRANCIS a couple of times. When the three figures arrive stage-left, BILLY takes gun from his back pocket and flings it into 'the lake'. A plash sound is heard followed by the flapping of a swan's wings. They carry on dragging the dead body of JOHN-JOE off stage, i.e. off to Aiken's Lake.

SCENE TWELVE

A few weeks later. Tidy but half-empty mobile home. The piano is outside. A light breeze blows through the room. A newspaper rattles, a few pages strewn around the room. Enter JOSIE carrying a bunch of wild flowers, with FRANCIS. She stops by the doorway and picks up the Angel holy-water font and feels inside.

JOSIE It's dry.

FRANCIS We stopped putting water in that thing a long time ago.

JOSIE Still, it's a nice thing. An angel. Maybe we'll take that.

FRANCIS Aye.

JOSIE wraps the angel in the newspaper. FRANCIS is distracted.

JOSIE Penny for your thoughts.

FRANCIS Oh I, I just thought that I shouldn't have let you ... I shoulda been the one ta, ya know ... do the deed, not you.

JOSIE No, Francie. You couldn't. You're a naturalist and naturalists don't shoot people. Leave it at that now. *(Beat.)* Though isn't it a good job Billy had enough skill to take that bullet out of his shoulder? I'm glad of that. I wouldn't have wanted to kill him.

FRANCIS No.

JOSIE And I'm glad John-Joe got his bus. Must have been in a bit of pain. Though I can't say I care.

FRANCIS Aye.

Beat.

JOSIE Francis, there's still a few boxes in the rooms. Have ya been through that stuff?

FRANCIS Only oul things from before. Her things. We won't be needin' them now.

JOSIE Where is he anyway?

FRANCIS Billy?

JOSIE Of course Billy.

FRANCIS Oh. He's down the swannery. He'll come up and we'll shift that piano up ta the house then.

JOSIE The swannery? Why's he down there?

FRANCIS Oh. He says something is caught up. Entangled in the reeds, and he a, he needs ta clear it or the swans won't go back ta nest. That's what he says, anyway.

JOSIE Well, Billy is the animal man.

FRANCIS That's it. Billy will sort it. Billy is the animal man. Oh, you'll want ta see him with the lambs and the calves, Josie. What an expert. But you'll see all that come spring.

JOSIE What was it got – entangled? Did he say?

FRANCIS Just some netting most likely. It happens. Fisherman using oul nets instead a lines, hopin' for a big haul. Aiken's is full of bream and tench and trout. Netting Josie, Netting. That or something thrown in. Some unwanted thing, maybe. That's all it is.

JOSIE is in and out of the rooms with boxes. She comes out with one box – full of books and records and places on the table. An album in the box catches her eye. She reads the song-list. Opens up the stereo, which is still there – and plays 'Martha' from 'Closing Time' by Tom Waits. When he hears the music, FRANCIS goes to stand by the doorway, looks out. Over the music, JOSIE talks:

JOSIE Which room did she sleep in, your mother?

FRANCIS One down. In mine.

Pause.

JOSIE Ya know Francis, things happen to people in families. Not always their fault, ya know? The weak lean on the strong. They lean and lean until sometimes the strong break – and then everyone is weak.

FRANCIS When I came back here in those first few months it was Billy who fed me, walked me, talked to me. She – was always lookin' on, lookin' out. It was Billy's voice kept me on this earth at all. His voice. Not hers. Because for a long time after Long Kesh, Josie – I was ...like Billy said, I was ... stranded, you know.

JOSIE Aye. And weren't we all that one time, Francis? Weren't we all?

FADE LIGHTS OVER MUSIC.

SCENE THIRTEEN

Sometime later. JOSIE, BILLY, FRANCIS are standing on the hill of Sloane's old house, looking down at the mobile home. Behind them the new wall of the old house. They are watching the mobile home burn.

FRANCIS It will be the best thing ever happened that field. The hot ash will do the land the world of good and we'll put horses on it when the grass grows. Next year maybe.

BILLY Glad to be out of it, tell ya that.

JOSIE Gave me great peace that little place. The best I've ever known.

FRANCIS Time we all moved on from it, I think.

BILLY Aye. It is.

JOSIE Did we really have to burn it though?

FRANCIS Best ta leave no trace. No trace of the thing at all.

BILLY Aye. It's called burning your bridges.

FRANCIS It will, more than anything else, Josie, be an entirely different life up here. We will have an understanding to reach. A sharing. Of this house, and of all we have. Because none of us really owns anything, as the American Indians used ta believe. It won't be easy, but it will be better than that Billy, eh?

Better than all that down there. Where we sank back on ourselves, huh? Oh my. Look at it burn.

JOSIE You think we can be happy, knowing what people will think of us up here?

BILLY People? What do we care? People have always hated the Sloanes. Sloanes, Gallaghers. They've got to hate someone. And who are they anyway, these people? I see no one. Only us three. Up on this hill.

FRANCIS Humbug to them all. It's a new beginning.

JOSIE And John-Joe? How will I ever forget shooting John-Joe, tell me? And me a vegan.

BILLY Didn't I see ta John-Joe? You have no need to worry about him, that's for sure.

FRANCIS Aye. Ya've no need to worry. John-Joe Doherty is probably holed up in some bar in London or Birmingham at this very moment. Probably tellin' a load a lies too, Josie, as to why he has a hole in his shoulder. He certainly won't be tellin' anyone that a woman done it to him in a caravan in the back a beyond. A caravan he was about to rob, too! That is not a good picture to be puttin' in anyone's head if ya want ta impress them. As one does in a bar in London or Birmingham. So don't you worry about that now, Josie. Ya won't be hearing from Joey the Lip again. I can absolutely guarantee it.

JOSIE It's a mobile home, Francis.

FRANCIS Who cares what it is. It's on fire! That's what it is. And about time too. And I'm tellin' ya Josie, had ya not done it, someone'd done it, he'd have got you inta that car, driven ya halfway between here and wherever he was goin', and he may well have bumped you off. He's a fool. But there's nothin' more dangerous than a fool with a gun. I for one can live with a hole in John-Joe's shoulder. *(Looks over at BILLY)*

BILLY Hear, hear. You were just defendin' a man who made a promise, Josie. I was a witness. I saw.

JOSIE I put a bullet in a man! It does not feel good.

BILLY You will just have ta live with it, Josie. As we all will.

JOSIE Look, a car's pulled up by the wee bridge. Who could that be I wonder?

FRANCIS Probably just some tourist, come to stop and take in the beauty of the place.

JOSIE You manage ta sort out that swan's nest, Billy?

BILLY Oh aye. *(BILLY glances at FRANCIS)*

JOSIE What was it got entangled? Was it netting?

BILLY Ah, no. It was nothin'. Only the bones of some lost animal. They do fall in and get stuck between the rocks. *(And for FRANCIS' attention in particular.)* Can take years sometimes for things at the end of that lake to rise up. Years and years and years.

FRANCIS Ya know we came close there ta losin' all of this. All this wonder and peace. Like a spell that would have been so easy to undo. *(There is a flapping sound; FRANCIS looks up)* There Josie! *(She doesn't look. And BILLY is looking at the mobile home burn)* There they go, the swans! Coming back to Aiken's now Billy has cleared the nest and they'll settle there for the winter. Look at that wingspan! A sight to behold. It'll be getting cold soon, and all of this land will change to white. Ready to begin again in spring. And I was thinking, Josie, and Billy, of planting some sapling lime trees along the pathway there. Then in the Mays to come we'd have the yellow blossom all before us. The lime tree is the tree to plant; the way the sun shines through the thin leaves. All in front like, so we'd see the sun filterin' through when we'd look out of this house. Eighteen, I was thinking. Seems like a nice number, and a nice thing to give back to the land. What d'ya think, eh? Josie – and Billy? *(BILLY continues to watch the mobile home burn; JOSIE eyes the car)* And years from now, when we are gone and this house is nothin' but old stones, those trees will be the only trace left of us. Though, who knows, someone might remember there were people up here; strange fish who lived by their own rules, but who tried to be true and did their best to be good. For the brief time they were on this earth.

JOSIE Oh, she seems so familiar to me, that woman.

BILLY Look at it burn! Look at it burn!

THE END.

photo credit: Colleen Clinton

Aurora Metro Books

HAMLET adapted by Mark Norfolk
ISBN 978-1-911501-01-5 £9.99

COMBUSTION by Asif Khan
ISBN 978-1-911501-91-6 £9.99

DIARY OF A HOUNSLOW GIRL by Ambreen Razia
ISBN 978-0-9536757-9-1 £8.99

SPLIT/MIXED by Ery Nzaramba
ISBN 978-1-911501-97-8 £10.99

A GIRL WITH A BOOK by Nick Wood
ISBN 978-1-910798-61-4 £12.99

THE TROUBLE WITH ASIAN MEN by Sudha Bhuchar, Kristine Landon-Smith and Louise Wallinger
ISBN 978-1-906582-41-8 £8.99

SOUTHEAST ASIAN PLAYS ed. Cheryl Robson and Aubrey Mellor
ISBN 978-1-906582-86-9 £16.99

SIX PLAYS BY BLACK AND ASIAN WOMEN WRITERS ed. Kadija George
ISBN 978-0-9515877-2-0 £12.99

DURBAN DIALOGUES, INDIAN VOICE by Ashwin Singh
ISBN 978-1-906582-42-5 £15.99

WOMEN OF ASIA by Asa Palomera
ISBN 978-1-906582-94-4 £7.99

HARVEST by Manjula Padmanabhan
ISBN 978-0-9536757-7-7 £6.99

I HAVE BEFORE ME A REMARKABLE DOCUMENT by Sonja Linden
ISBN 978-0-9546912-3-3 £7.99

THE IRANIAN FEAST by Kevin Dyer
ISBN 978-1-910798-93-5 £8.99

NEW SOUTH AFRICAN PLAYS ed. Charles J. Fourie
ISBN 978-0-9542330-1-3 £11.99

BLACK AND ASIAN PLAYS Anthology introduced by Afia Nkrumah
ISBN 978-0-9536757-4-6 £12.99

www.aurorametro.com